Life on the Allegheny Plateau

*An immigrant coal miner's son
grows up in Hillbilly America*

Edward W. Jedrziewski

ROOTS IN MYTH, AUSTIN, TX

This book is based on the personal experiences of the author and accurately describes life on the eastern Allegheny Plateau from about 1930 to 1950.

For the most part, names of people are not used in order to respect the memory of those who have departed and to avoid potential embarrassment to the living. Where names are used, they have been fictionalized except for those of the author's immediate family.

All photographs are from family archives.

Life on the Allegheny Plateau
An Immigrant Coal Miner's Son Grows Up in Hillbilly America

Copyright © 2022 by Edward W. Jedrziewski
All rights reserved.

For more information, contact:
Roots in Myth
Austin, TX
roots@rootsinmyth.com
www.rootsinmyth.com

All rights reserved. This book may not be reproduced in any manner whatsoever without express permission of the copyright holder.

ISBN: 978-1-949717-36-5 (trade paperback)

First trade paperback edition: December 2022

This book is dedicated to the brave immigrants who came to America in the latter part of the 19th century and the early 20th century. The courage shown by these people who, for the most part, left their homes and families never to return is exemplary.

They entered a land and culture that was foreign to them but worked hard and assimilated to the extent possible while maintaining their ethnic identity. The foundations they laid allowed many of their offspring to become part of the American dream.

In particular, this book is dedicated to my parents and siblings, who had a lot of hard rows to hoe in pursuit of the dream.

Table of Contents

Basic Instincts	3
The Probabilities of Birth	7
New Fertile Ground	12
A Grand Entrance	18
My World	27
A Glimpse of the World Beyond	35
The Food Chain	38
The Great Depression	44
Social Customs and Religion	51
Figures of Speech	73
The Village Store	80
The Kitchen Stove	83
Tilling the Soil	87
Butchering Time	95
The Robins of My Youth	101
The Great Strawberry Raid	104
Theft in the Village	107
Horse Theft	110
Outhouses	114
A Cow Named Lady	117
An Easy Place	122
A Few Bricks Shy of a Full Load	129

The Games Men Play	133
By Any Other Name	139
An Early Interest in Automobiles	142
A Spirit of Adventure	147
Small Game Hunting	151
The Boys and the Deer	153
The Resilience of Nature	163
Angels and Mean-Spirited Bitches	172
The Age of Enlightenment	198
A World War II Experience	206
A New Journey Begins	225

Judge people not only by the destinations reached in their journeys through life but also by the starting points and the roads traveled.

Chapter 1
Basic Instincts

I sat in the outhouse with the door open because it was a hot summer day. The gentle breeze from the northwest felt good and took the odor out through the knotholes and gaps between the rough sawn pine boards. Fortunately, the flies were not a problem because they preferred the manure pile behind the nearby barn, which was a village landmark because two of the sides were painted with Mail Pouch Chewing Tobacco signs.

When I was finished, I wiped using a couple of the soft index pages from the Sears Roebuck catalog. There were still quite a few of these left, so the unpleasant task of using the slick color pages could wait a while.

While I was buttoning my pants, I glanced out beyond our pigpen, vegetable garden, and barbed wire fence that was the boundary between our property and that of the neighbor. I could see him hoeing his garden located beyond a small hayfield.

The distance between us was about 200 feet, which gave him privacy in the sense that he was not expected to wave to me or acknowledge in any manner that we saw each other. In our valley, people working outdoors did not speak to each other unless they were about 20 feet apart. They just went about their business. If they were serious about their current task, subtle hints of body language let them keep their privacy even if someone was nearby.

He was a ruddy-faced Irishman with a twinkle in his eyes. Our family got along well with him, possibly because we shared a common love of the land. His probably started when the Irish came to America to escape the potato famine. Knowing that starving to death was a real possibility created a nearly genetic affection for all edible plants.

He had inherited the land and house from his mother, whom he had taken care of until her death about two years earlier. He then married one of the local girls, who lived across the road from us. They were both in their forties and seemed suited for each other.

Prior to getting married, he was drafted into the army about halfway through World War II. Everyone thought he would make an unlikely soldier, and there was a lot of talk about the draft board pulling some kind of political move, because by going into the army, he lost his job as township road supervisor.

In fact, he did not make it through basic training, and I recall him coming home and getting off the bus near our house. He had a wrinkled uniform, apparently from long and hot travel.

He hoed the garden in a manner befitting one with a lot of experience. First, the garden was fairly large, so there was no point in trying to rush through the job. Like most people descended from peasantry, the way you did the job was more important than how quickly you did it.

A few chops with the hoe were followed by leaning over and pulling the weeds that had been loosened. They were next tapped against the hoe to make sure that the precious soil remained in the garden, and then tossed into the grassy area nearby, where they would decay and be spaded into the soil the next year.

An experienced hoer was also accustomed to working all day. This was probably a carryover from the times when people worked for a lord with an estate, so there was no motivation to do a job quickly. If you finished one job and it was still daylight, you were given something else to do. The concept of "finding a pace that you can hold" was probably invented here.

While the hoeing and weeding were going on, the neighbor's wife walked down from the house and sat near the garden on a stacked and covered pile of old lumber. When the neighbor was asked about this pile, he stated that it was for a future project. It became a bit of a joke in the neighborhood that the project was undetermined and far in the future.

I could see that the wife was talking to her husband as he worked. He glanced at her occasionally but kept working at the same pace. She then pulled the skirt of her dress up to her hips and he stopped hoeing but leaned on the hoe and carried on a conversation. Even at the distance I was looking from, you could tell that she had nothing on under the dress.

She then spread her legs, and he dropped the hoe. After about a half minute, she started walking up toward the house and he followed. As they neared the building, their pace quickened, and they disappeared inside.

I was eleven years old at the time and had a very general idea of what was about to transpire but was severely lacking in specifics. Being a farm boy, I had observed our animals performing primitive functions, but it was a bit strange to visualize humans doing something similar.

In later years, I would wonder how I came to be in this place at this time, and the possibilities were truly mind-boggling. I eventually reached the conclusion that the path of a human through life is determined by a remarkable sequence of conditional probabilities, and that people are the most amazing thing on the earth. I would also conclude that civilization is a thin and extremely fragile veneer that regulates behavior, which, if left unchecked, would include nearly everything imaginable.

Chapter 2
The Probabilities of Birth

If you try to visualize the total number of human eggs produced during the existence of humans, it becomes a number beyond comprehension. If you do the same with sperm, it is even more mind-boggling. The probability of having any one egg meet any one sperm is likely beyond the capability of a meaningful computation.

When you add geographical location to probability, it becomes even more complex, and the possibilities are endless. However, the total process is self-sustaining and occurs naturally. I once read that it is remarkable that such a complex event is performed by unskilled labor.

Any one person could have been conceived and born into greatly varying circumstances. At the one extreme, you have poverty, pestilence, and suffering and at the other, you have wealth and privilege. Physical and mental attributes and handicaps add to the possibilities and cover the whole spectrum.

Regardless of the circumstances into which people are born, all have one thing in common. Everyone ever conceived and born had absolutely no influence or control over where, when, or how the event occurred. In poker parlance, it is like trying to win the game with the first and only hand that would be dealt to you.

My egg came from a Polish peasant immigrant girl who came to this country in the early 20th century. Her family were landowners. Being a female, she did not inherit land and was expected to marry someone who did.

The way she told it, her marriage prospects were with ancient widowers, so she came to America in search of something better. Some of her brothers were here already working in the coal mines near Johnstown, Pennsylvania, and she joined them.

Her port of entry was Baltimore, and she told the story of being petrified when she saw her first black man who laughed when she started shrieking.

She lived with her brothers in Johnstown and got a job as a cleaning woman in a hospital with a wage of about fifty cents a week. She worked at this job for only about a year, and then my father came along and changed her life.

My father left Poland by himself when he was seventeen years old. His family did not own land, but worked for a lord. He sometimes told the story of walking with his father to a guide that would lead him over the Polish border into Germany, and knowing that it was the last time they would ever see each other.

He described the ship journey as a terrifying experience with rough seas and a lot of "mal de mer." Being in steerage class, lunch sometimes consisted of a crew member opening a keg of salted herrings, which the passengers ate but then developed an insatiable thirst as a result.

He had relatives in Philadelphia and joined them after going through the whole Ellis Island experience. Without knowing a word of English, he somehow was able to make a train journey. I can only assume that someone had sent him some instructions, which he had to memorize because he could not read.

He worked as a stevedore for a while and described unloading rough sawn lumber from barges that had been brought down the Delaware river. This was his first exposure to tides, and he was amazed that on some days the barges were sitting on the bottom.

He took a better-paying job as a leather ironer in a tannery. The work consisted of hot ironing hides that had been soaked in a dyeing vat. The object was to get them shiny on the smooth side so that they could be used for making things like shoes. He talked about having hands that were perpetually black.

Even though life was hard, it was better than the

existence he had on an estate in Poland. For the first time, he had freedom when he was not at work. In his old life, the lord of the estate treated people as though he owned them 24 hours a day.

He talked of simple pleasures like getting a bucket of beer on a hot sweltering evening, eating raw oysters for the first time, and the camaraderie he felt with the relatives that were providing a place to live and teaching him English, reading, writing, and basic arithmetic.

He talked about the racial tension that existed between the immigrants and the black population. This did not present much of a problem because the tough working Polack boys could give as well as they got, so the few minor altercations generally ended in truces. Possibly, there was a feeling of empathy because each group was being exploited by the WASPs.

The immigrants had developed a job opportunity network, and he heard about better-paying jobs in the soft coal region of Pennsylvania. He took advantage of an offer to go to the mines near Johnstown as a "greenhorn" working with an experienced miner. A greenhorn did all the basic physical work until he got enough experience to get a "place" of his own and then got his own greenhorn.

Purely as a result of fate, he worked in the same mine where my mother's brothers did. They introduced her to my father, and after a short courtship, they were married in Johnstown. My father was a thrifty man and paid all wedding expenses, including the cost of the dress for the bride. They got some gold plated brass wedding bands.

City life, especially in low grade mining town housing, did not appeal to them, so they took advantage of an opportunity to move to the Appalachian mountain region of central Pennsylvania, where he continued his mining occupation. He developed his mining skills and served as an apprentice to the operator of a coal undercutting machine and then became the chief cutter.

Where they happened to settle is an interesting place with a lot of geological history. It is far from the plains of Poland, but they made a life that retained a lot of the same roots.

Thus, the conditional probabilities of my birth included the willingness of two people to have the courage to leave their native soil, move to a land of opportunity and unknowns, meet by chance, and settle into what some people would consider to be the middle of nowhere.

Chapter 3
New Fertile Ground

The Appalachian Mountains of central Pennsylvania were formed about 500 million years ago, give or take a few minutes, when all of the continents collided and formed a master land mass called Pangaea. Subsequent separations, collisions, and erosion formed what we ended up with today.

The eastern part of central Pennsylvania consists of a series of sharp ridges and valleys, with fertile farmland in the low lands. The western area is delineated by a sharp ridge called the Allegheny Front, and the region west of there is called the Allegheny Plateau.

When viewed from above, the Allegheny Front sticks out as a sharp dividing line between the two regions, and the differing resources of the areas resulted in a marked difference in cultures. The ridge and valley region became dominated by prosperous farms, limestone quarries, and manufacturing, and the plateau land was the source of timber and minerals such as coal and clay. The local clay was made into bricks, primarily the kind used in steel mills.

The Bald Eagle valley is at the eastern edge of the Allegheny Front, and has, from south to north, settlements with names like Altoona, Tipton, Tyrone, Bald Eagle, and Port Matilda. To the east of the valley, you find the town of State College and Penn State University.

When the Appalachian mountains first formed, they were a bit higher than the Himalayas, or about 30 thousand feet in elevation. Erosion over a period of 500 million years resulted in the 2000 to 3000 feet timbered hills that we now have. At first, this seems impossible to believe, but some simple arithmetic shows that they needed to erode at an average rate of less than one thousandth of an inch per year, which in one lifetime would not even be perceptible. In their current state, erosion is nearly nonexistent because the decaying vegetation replenishes the soil.

When I was a child in the region, simple minds had trouble even comprehending erosion. One neighbor nicknamed Doc, a descendant of the original settlers, expressed disbelief when I once talked about the starting elevation and erosion to the current state. His explanation was that "The land was the way it is now because that was the way the Good Lord made it and it was always like that." He used the same rationale for the coal being in the ground and could not comprehend that it was once vegetation.

The geographical position where my conditional probabilities landed me was slightly to the west of the Allegheny Front at the eastern end of the bituminous coal region. The towns and villages of the region have names like Frugality, Dean, Dysart, Fallen Timber, Glasgow, Glen Hope, Smoke Run, Osceola Mills, Chester Hill, Sandy Ridge, and Snowshoe. The names were bestowed by the early settlers who moved into the area after the Revolutionary War.

The topography of the region varies greatly in a short distance. The highest elevation of the Allegheny Front is rocky soil that has stunted trees, scrub oak, ferns, mountain laurel, and blueberry and huckleberry plants. There is a lot of an aromatic shrub called sweet fern. Little farming was done at this elevation because better land existed as you went down in elevation to the west.

As you drop down and head west, you encounter springs that start to form streams. As you descend farther, additional springs contribute to the flow that provides a source of water for the small towns. The excess water continues and joins with other tributaries that initially flow westward, then north, and join an east-flowing branch of the Susquehanna River that finally flows into the Chesapeake Bay and the Atlantic. If you stood near a spring with moss-covered rocks and tried to explain this to Doc, he would look at you with disbelief.

In Appalachian parlance, "hollows" are the basic eroded areas that lead to "runs" which join "valleys." Hollows may be either dry or have water, but runs and valleys always have streams. In the valley, a stream is called a creek, or *crick* in local parlance. Creeks eventually join rivers.

The higher elevations frequently have clusters of rocks, which were apparently deposited as the mountains eroded. In the distance of a few miles down hill, the only rocks are under the soil.

Dropping down, the trees increase in size and include varieties of oak and maple. Rhododendron and mountain laurel both exist. Sassafras is encountered in the higher elevations but is nearly nonexistent lower down.

When you get to the eastern edge of the soft coal region, the water becomes polluted from mine drainage, but the soil becomes more fertile, and the trees are larger. This is the area that held the old growth pines and hemlocks that formed the basis for a booming timber industry in the 1800s. When these were harvested, the oaks and maples generated and provided a continuing source of renewable raw material.

The place where I was born and lived until I was 21 years old is about five miles west of the highest point on the Allegheny Front. It is roughly where the bottomland near the streams becomes large enough to grow crops, but not large enough for serious farming.

The valley where our home was located had a polluted stream and some working coalmines in the hillsides. There were some swampy areas that had aspen trees and small cranberry bogs. In the springtime, the peeper frogs made a nighttime melody that is hard to forget.

The area was sparsely settled until harvesting of the virgin pines and hemlocks became a booming industry in the 1800s. Later, when coal mining and the expansion of railroads required more labor, the population grew and reached a peak during the war years of the 1940s.

The ethnic mix changed along with the industries. Timber harvesting was done mostly by settlers of English and German stock, but coal mining and railroading brought in large numbers of Irish, Poles, Russians, Slovaks, and Lithuanians. The owners of the brickyards brought in some Negro labor, but blacks never became a significant part of the population, and when the brickyards closed, most migrated to the larger cities.

I came into the world the same year that Franklin Roosevelt was first elected president. This was a time when Model T Fords were common, a Model A was considered to be a relatively new car, and you could find cars with names like Essex, Whippet, Hupmobile, DeSoto, Lasalle, Hudson, and Packard.

Radio was a fairly new link to the outside world, and not every household had one. Much of what was known by an individual was communicated by a neighbor or by conversation in the many ethnic social and benevolent clubs. The churches were major centers of community life, and religion helped form many opinions.

Breastfeeding of babies was common, and disposable diapers were unknown. On the small farms, edible garbage was fed to the pigs, combustible trash was burned in the kitchen stove, used cans were put to use as containers for starting seedlings or storing nails, nuts, and bolts. Bottles were returned to vendors for refilling or used for treats such as homemade root beer.

However, it was not an ecological utopia. The great number of pigsties, manure piles, drainage ditches, and outhouses produced aromas and a crop of flies that would invade the houses and darken the porches when the weather turned cold. Flypaper was a common item in grocery and hardware stores, as were rat traps. Refrigeration was uncommon, and perishable food was eaten within a day of being brought home from the store.

Compared to the early 21st century, it was both culturally and materially a different kind of world.

Chapter 4
A Grand Entrance

At five o'clock in the morning in early January of 1932, the year Franklin Roosevelt was first elected president, with the temperature near zero and snow on the ground, I came into the world in an unheated second-story bedroom. The birth was uncomplicated, my mother having experienced eight previous children.

A doctor was in attendance, having driven to the house in his second car, a new Ford V8. This was the first year that the V8 was produced and it was widely discussed as a technological marvel. It would gain additional fame when it became the car of choice for Clyde Barrow of *Bonnie and Clyde* notoriety.

After tying off the umbilical cord and making sure that my mother was in good hands, the doctor charged my father the princely sum of five dollars. He was paid with a gold back bill of the type that was slowly disappearing from circulation. He was amazed that my father had such money, it being the bottom of the great depression. Later, he would tell the story around town that he really didn't expect to get paid and showed the bill as an example of what was possible with hard work and thrift.

The presence at birth was the first time my mother had seen a doctor during the entire pregnancy. The concept of medical insurance and so-called health care was as foreign to her world as aliens from another planet. Her prenatal care consisted of common sense nutrition, no smoking, drinking only on ceremonial occasions, and a lot of exercise from hard work as a farm housewife. Good genes inherited from ancestors who had been subjected to survival of the fittest also helped.

My immigrant parents had no formal education. My mother was taught to read by her mother in a two-room dirt floored cottage on the plains of Poland. She never learned to write anything except her signature, which she would practice for hours. However, she had an excellent memory and could recite many prayers and a lot of lore passed on by her mother.

My father went to a formal school for one winter while the Russians occupied Poland. He did not learn to read or write until he came to America, where his aunt in Philadelphia taught him reading, writing, addition, and subtraction. He knew nothing of multiplication or division, and I recall him adding a whole column of the same number to get a multiple.

Based on their observation of the world around them in America, both recognized the value of learning. They worked hard, saved their money, and instilled hope in their children that a better life awaited them if they studied and got an education.

Both my mother and father always had difficulty adapting their culture to that of the new world and viewed many of the local ways with suspicion. They had been brought up in a rigorous Catholic faith that stressed morality and the avoidance of sin. The world they saw around them was opposite to everything they had been taught. They sheltered their children from influences that they considered both godless and foreign. I recall that one of the strongest admonitions was "You don't want to be like so and so, do you?" when observing some reprehensible behavior by someone in the neighborhood.

I grew up in what would now be considered extreme poverty. However, I did not go hungry and had a two-parent family who did not even consider divorce. Looking back on my childhood, I am convinced that poverty is as much a state of mind as it is an absence of material goods.

Some of my early memories include the feeling of warmth and comfort from sleeping between my parents under a feather tick pierzyna. Using a pierzyna is a sleeping experience like no other. The collection of feathers and down, about one foot thick, settles over the sleeper like the walls of a womb. If used in a cold bedroom, the feeling of coziness promotes a carefree sleep of total relaxation. It is somewhat the same feeling that you get at an isolated beach with your eyes closed listening to the surf—another womb related experience that leads to interesting speculation when you hear the crash of a large wave on the shore.

At a tender age

Pierzyni in the Slavic culture are a prized possession and passed down to each generation. They are considered to be a prestigious gift for a new bride. The work involved in making one is substantial, with down and feathers carefully stripped of any quills. In my family, stripping feathers was a typical winter evening pastime before the age of radio and television.

Even though my mother came to this country unmarried, she brought a pierzyna with her. It is still in the family and is now owned by one of her daughters.

Barefoot with new bib overalls which were a gift from an aunt

I was told that I imitated the sound of a steam engine when six months old. My mother told me about this often and thought it was some kind of sign of exceptional intelligence. Of course, at a young age, I did not contradict her.

I remember going barefoot in summer, not because I wanted to but because I had no shoes. When I was about four, some of the older kids were going to the woods to find the cows because they had not yet come home. I wanted to go, but they said I couldn't because I had no shoes and my feet would get cut. I went into the cellar and found some old shoes that were too big and had almost no bottoms, put them on although my bare feet touched the ground through them, but went to the woods.

I got my first pair of new shoes when starting into the second grade and remembered being proud of them. The only unpleasant thing was that from that point on, when I got new shoes, I had to kiss my father's hand to show thanks. This custom continued until I was well into my teens, and one day I refused to do it. My father didn't press the issue, although he didn't like what he considered to be a sign of disrespect.

The first time I saw a doctor after birth was to get a smallpox vaccination before starting first grade. This was in the days when the vaccination was performed to intentionally leave a scar as testimony to the fact that it had been done.

There were happy times in my childhood. I had pleasant memories of waking up to the sound of a butter churn thumping in the kitchen below, the smell of fresh baking bread and cinnamon buns, and the taste of fresh bread with new butter and homemade jelly.

In later years, I had memories of being happy when my mother baked a birthday cake especially for me. After World War II started, and my father was working regularly again, my mother would bake good cookies. I remember their taste after coming home from school.

Pants rolled up and proud of my first new shoes

My mother also made a fantastic bean soup. It was made only in the summer time and used all fresh ingredients: green and yellow beans, carrots, and new potatoes. It was creamed with fresh milk that came from our cows.

As a child, I learned anatomy from butchering farm animals, and the similarity of the hog to humans was apparent at an early age. Sex education was learned from watching the animals and from talk with older children, and later it became one of my jobs to lead the cows to a breed bull. Naturally, I watched the whole operation with great interest.

There are memories of the sound of bells when the cows were being driven to the woods for the day and when they came home at night, the music of peeper frogs on a spring evening, the crowing of roosters in the morning, the wonder of seeing chicks being hatched, the births of calves, the taste of boiled freshly picked sweet corn smothered in new butter, the taste of a freshly picked vine-ripened tomato, and the vast expanse of the woods as a playground and a place to explore.

The woods near the farm provided pleasures like fresh wild strawberries, blueberries, and blackberries. In the fall, there were hickory nuts and wild grapes.

The Appalachian wild flowers in the spring are awesome, and the scent of flowering apple trees is something that you never forget. In the summer, the beauty and power of an evening thunderstorm over the hills was a wonder to behold, and the echoes of thunder in the valleys and hollows was a sound never heard in the flatlands.

Nature and plants and animals have always been a large part of my life. I was awed by the magnificence of all natural things and to this day am moved by such things as looking out over a landscape of fall colors. Hunting and the woods experience are things that I enjoy even now.

Religion played a big part in forming my values. In later years, when asked if any one person had a major influence on my life, I could think of no one. As I pondered the question, I came to the conclusion that Jesus Christ, and his teachings as communicated in the gospels read at Mass each Sunday, provided much of the wisdom that guided me through life.

I grew up believing that being close to nature brings you close to God. When alone in the woods in any season, I still get a spiritual feeling, and I thank God that I have been given an opportunity to experience life on this earth.

Chapter 5
My World

My world was quite small, but as a child, it seemed large to me. Our house was in a strung out village of small irregular lots in a mountain valley. A stream polluted by coal mine drainage ran through it, and the old timers told of better days when you could catch trout there.

My world in 1939

The lots and houses were on either side of a road that wound its way through the valley. One side of the road had a well-used foot path, because cars were rare and walking was a way of life. For some unknown reason, only one side was used, and a stranger could be immediately spotted if he walked on the "wrong side."

Looking south in winter. The small buildings near the road are coal shanties for storing fuel.

Looking from the house in all directions, you couldn't see more than a few hundred yards. On one side of the valley, across the stream, were some abandoned coal mines nestled on a hillside in a hardwood forest. On the other steeper side, the hilly lots were topped by a double track railroad that was used for hauling coal to the east. From the east, the empty coal cars returned, along with freight that was used in the area.

When the sun rose in the morning, you could look

west and see the bright rays first illuminate the hilltops and then slowly work their way down to the valley as life began to stir. Smoke from wood and coal-burning kitchen ranges floated along the stream bottom until the air warmed and caused it to rise toward the sky.

In the evening, the process was reversed. The setting sun brought shadows to the valley long before evening, and the cooling air and smoke settled into the *crick* bottom. Gradually, a mist began to form above the fields in the summer, and in winter, the sun-melted slush began to refreeze.

My home was on the stream side of the road, where the farm land was better. All tillable areas were farmed to some extent, but the only serious growers were on the stream side. The rocks on the hilly side proved to be too much, even for the hardy settlers. Where the land had been seriously cleared, the fencerows were lined with stones that had been picked from the soil.

The valley was originally settled by people of English ancestry, who moved to the area when harvesting of the virgin pines and hemlocks began. When the wave of Slav and Irish immigrants arrived, they referred to the initial wave as *Johnny Bulls*, a name which endured until the ethnic mix made it irrelevant.

The original settlers slowly adopted a lifestyle of no ambition, "stay where you are and take what life gives to you," "work only when it was convenient or you were compelled to do so," and "exist on as little as possible." This philosophy contributed to a gradual decline, which eventually led to the group losing its identity.

Looking north in summer. Everything was farmed.

The lack of mobility led to a lot of intermarriage, which, when coupled with offspring that were the result of extracurricular activity, seriously depleted the gene pool to the extent that there was some physical and mental deformity by the time of this story. Nature, in her infinite wisdom, would correct this problem.

Large families were not the norm in this group. The newcomers later wondered how the Johnny Bulls would do this and speculated that there was a lot of coitus interruptus going on, or maybe it was a lot of doing without.

Being "on relief" was the norm for a large part of this group. With the air of superiority that they had, they considered this an entitlement and nothing to be ashamed of and would look down on the new immigrants who toiled in their fields and worked hard at the coal mining jobs that they were grateful to have.

The immigrants who moved into the area in the late 1800s and early 1900s consisted of Irish and eastern Europeans of various nationalities. The Irish worked in the coalmines and on the railroad, and the Slavs worked in the coal mines. The newcomers would change the valley and the population.

The immigrants first lived in substandard rental houses in the nearby town. For the most part, they were frugal, and as soon as they could afford to do so, they bought small plots in the valley and erected modest houses. Being of peasant origin, they were naturally drawn to the land where they could follow the lifestyle they had left behind. The ability and desire to work hard was a characteristic they brought with them.

As the newcomers settled into their way of life in the valley, it immediately generated ethnic conflict. The Johnny Bulls looked down on them for all the apparently needless hard work they did, the funny names the Slavs had, the large families that were common, and for their self-reliance. It was unheard of for an immigrant family to go "on relief." The great depression would later change this, but initially the differences between the haves and the have-nots did not contribute to harmony.

My first memories of this were being called a hunky,

a derogatory term applied to all the Slavs. Even in what was supposed to be polite conversation, subtle references to large families being like a "bunch of rabbits" were made, with the idea that the Johnny Bulls somehow were better because they had fewer kids.

Human nature being what it is, the children of different backgrounds played together, and you could tell what their parents believed by the comments of the kids. People didn't cross ethnic lines to visit in each other's homes, but you could gain some insight by how the kids talked. On one occasion, a three-year-old Johnny Bull boy with a broken tricycle blamed it on "this goddamn screw is broke."

Compared to the immigrants, religion among the Johnny Bulls was not organized. Few went to a church, and home prayer meetings and bible study were substituted. This style of worship probably originated when they first moved to the area, and there were no churches. Later, they probably did it out of habit and the view that supporting a church was a needless expense. Even funerals were conducted from the home, with simple prayers being said before the deceased was hauled off to the cemetery.

The organized religion of the immigrants was looked down upon, and dressing up to go to church was viewed as a bunch of silliness. Most of the locals didn't own a suit or even a white shirt, and I recall one, whom I earlier introduced as Doc, on a special occasion using his only stained necktie with a dull gray work shirt.

Doc was typical of the deteriorating breed. In the summer, he spent a lot of time lying in the shade under a tree, and in the winter he sat at a window looking out. His house had neither a front porch nor a back porch, so even his ability to goof off was limited by his lack of ambition. He had one pair of reading glasses that had a broken ear piece, which he jury-rigged with a piece of grocers twine looped around an ear. His only reading was a newspaper named the *Grit*.

I never knew him to have a job except during World War II, when the "relief" administrators had no sympathy for him. I recall him listening to Pittsburgh Pirates baseball games on the radio while we toiled in the fields. He frequently talked about something called the "Townsend Plan" which would pay everyone over sixty years of age a sum of $100 per month, which they would be required to spend in order to stimulate the economy. Something for nothing was definitely part of Doc's mentality.

By the time I was aware of things, the valley had changed to the point where the immigrants and their numerous offspring dominated it. They tilled most of the land, kept cows that they pastured in the surrounding woods, and improved their homes as they accumulated wealth. They seriously out-bred the Johnny Bulls, who were not aware that their days were numbered.

Hormones being what they are, some marriage took place between the immigrant females and the Johnny Bull males. Much later, some immigrant males married outside of their kind, but in lesser numbers than the females. I don't know the reason for this, but it may have something to do with male dominance. Invariably, the immigrant females gave up their religion for the sake of harmony. Besides, a self respecting Johnny Bull would not set foot inside a Catholic church.

The new gene pool was a welcome addition, and the offspring of these unions generally produced good looking children. Also, some of the immigrant work ethic was transferred, and these sons and daughters did well. In most cases, even the Johnny Bull fathers developed some ambition, which says a lot for the power of hormones and a nagging wife.

There were events on the horizon that would seriously change the balance between the ethnic groups, and they would happen in a relatively short period of time. The net result would be that the original settlers of English origin would disappear as an identifiable culture.

Chapter 6
A Glimpse of the World Beyond

My earliest memories of the world beyond my village are of a trip to Penn State in a Model A Ford. I was about five years old and recall my father driving two of my brothers there when the fall semester started. I was pleased to go along on my first big adventure. Going down the mountain on Route 350 was my first sensation of needing to pop my ears to relieve the pressure change as altitude dropped.

I recall that my father took the car out of gear and coasted on the lower part of the mountain in order to save gasoline. When we got to Bald Eagle, I saw why it was also called the Triangle, because of the way Route 350 split into two directions where it met Route 220.

Everything I saw in the Bald Eagle valley was new to me. The neat dairy farms and the tall corn in fields that were actually level. The climb up Skytop mountain took a long time, and we finally arrived at the university, called a college in those days. It was a place of neat buildings, wide sidewalks, elm trees, mowed lawns, and students bustling everywhere as they moved into the dorms. I remember being told that someday I would be part of this life.

I recall another trip down the mountain, this time to pick cherries at a dairy farm before you got to Bald Eagle. The farmer had a row of trees along a fencerow, and we picked cherries for our use and paid him about five cents per quart. Also, we got to eat as many as we wanted during the picking. It was both a novel and enjoyable experience. When we left, the ground was strewn with pits where we had spit them out while picking. The chipmunks probably stored them away for the winter in a few days.

This was my first close look at a dairy farm, and the barn and equipment were fascinating. For the first time, I saw lightning rods on a barn and asked about why they were there and how they worked.

A few years later, I remember a trip to Tyrone to pick up a sister at the train station when she came home from Philadelphia where she was a nursing student. It was my first exposure to the smell of the paper mill and the neat water sprays coming from the building. I had no envy for anyone that lived in a town with that kind of odor.

I had seen steam engines before in the hills, but the

ones at the stations were pulling passenger cars only, and a lot of people got on and off as we waited for my sister. A baggage cart with steel wheels was a new sight, and I was fascinated to see the baggage master wheel a load of luggage.

My first trip to Altoona was what I considered to be a visit to a really big city. The huge train station, tall buildings, and vast railroad yards were a sight to behold. The fact that steam engines were manufactured nearby was amazing to me, because I always assumed that they came from some mysterious place far away.

On the way to and from Altoona, we drove by the small airport at Tipton, and I got my first look at brightly colored airplanes on the ground and a few in the air. From that point on, I was fascinated with airplanes.

Trips from my valley were few and far between, and my life centered around the circumstances into which I had been born. The visions beyond were something to dream about.

Chapter 7
The Food Chain

The economy on the plateau started with the natural resources of the region. Everything began with coal, timber, and the clay used to make bricks. If it were not for these, the railroads and various supporting and service industries would not have existed.

If you were to draw a boundary around the region, the commodities that flowed outward were coal, lumber for the building and furniture industries, pulpwood for the paper mills in the more civilized regions to the east and to the west, and fire bricks for the steel industry in Pittsburgh. The money that flowed into the region from the sale of these commodities fueled a lifestyle that varied from extreme poverty at the one end to ostentatious wealth at the other.

It seemed that the nearer you were to the basic source of wealth, the deeper the poverty was. Stated another way, the bottom of the human food chain was located in the same place as the commodities that provided a luxurious lifestyle to others.

The poorest of the miners, who were mostly eastern European immigrants, lived in small isolated company towns. The houses were owned by the employer and rented to the workers. The buildings were of the cheapest construction possible, which consisted of posts instead of a foundation and walls made of vertical rough sawn boards.

The inside walls were finished with old newspaper glued to the boards with flour paste, and the floors were covered with various materials that were salvaged from elsewhere. There was no plumbing, water being obtained from community wells, and outhouses were used for other functions.

Disposal of dishwater and bath water was done by the "swoosh" method. This consisted of taking the dishpan or washtub to the door and on to any porch that existed and then "swooshing" it out onto the ground. Kitchen garbage and liquid chamber pot waste were handled in the same manner.

The chickens owned by the families roamed freely during the daytime and fed on whatever garbage and other food they found to their liking. At night they came home to roost in the chicken coops in which they had hatched. Some of the families kept dairy cows for their own use and to sell milk products to the others.

Heat and cooking were done with a coal-burning kitchen range. Furniture consisted of whatever could be made from rough lumber or handed down from someone else. Beds were uncommon, and the hardy souls slept on the floor with covers that apparently were adequate to keep from freezing to death in winter.

The company store existed in reality and was not a myth popularized by the Tennessee Ernie Ford song. The only way the miner could get out of debt to the store was to find a job outside of the company town and upgrade his lifestyle. The more ambitious did just that, but many accepted their lot in life and took what came their way, which was not much.

A one-room schoolhouse was provided in the isolated company towns by the township school board. The lone teacher was always male and ruled with an iron hand. Even the meanest of the mean-spirited spinster bitches from the larger consolidated schools would not have lasted a day in the presence of tough young lads who had been battle hardened by coping with adversity at all levels.

Discipline was more important than learning. After all, the teacher didn't need to work hard to teach a bunch of immigrants' children who would only quit school and work in the mines with their fathers. Most already did so on Saturdays and during the summer, and child labor laws existed in theory only.

The girls usually stayed in school a bit longer, but their usual ambition was to marry someone who could provide for them, hopefully in a manner better than they were accustomed to.

Workers benefits were a joke. There was no medical care of any kind except for government-mandated workman's compensation if the miner was injured. The non-union miners did not get any paid vacation or mandated paid holidays. The only pension was social security.

The miners were paid on the basis of what they produced in the way of finished coal, which they loaded on coal cars that sometimes were weighed and sometimes accounted for "by the car." Weighing was usually dishonest and an occasional car got counted for the "boss." If the miner protested, he was told that he could always leave to go work somewhere else.

The loggers were usually not immigrants but were descended from the old English stock that originally settled the area. They were either independent operators or worked for a larger timbering company. They did not live in company towns, but the poorest lived in one-story shacks that, for all intents and purposes, provided conditions like those in the company towns.

This was not the era of chainsaws, and cutting was done with a two-man crosscut saw that was pulled in each direction by a two-man crew. Limbs were removed with an ax. Cutting was done year-round in all conditions.

Pulpwood was peeled with an ax and loaded onto a truck by hand. At the mill, it was also unloaded by hand after being weighed. Locally, pulpwood was referred to as "poverty wood" because of the massive amount of labor needed for a modest payment.

If the logger didn't work, he didn't produce anything that he could sell to generate income. Workers benefits were about the same as those enjoyed by the miners—essentially none.

The brickyard operators usually imported Negro labor that they controlled in a company town that was about as degrading as that used in the coal operations. A two-room shack was provided for a family to live in. Politely phrased, these were locally called "Negro shanties."

Except for the isolated one-room schools in the company towns, the poor whites, the blacks, and the more affluent whites went to the same schools because separate schools could not be afforded. In a way, you could call this integration by economic necessity. Although it was not planned, it worked out to be a good way to accomplish something that human nature would not gracefully accept.

In spite of being at the bottom of the local food chain, the people led lives that had some happiness in them. They had their share of family disputes, domestic violence, child abuse, theft, and sickness. However, even in the face of adversity, they enjoyed the simple pleasures of each other's company and conversation, their religious values, and a culture that bonded those that were being exploited by others.

They prepared simple but nutritious food, much of which was grown in small garden patches among their houses. They carried on the traditions of the eastern European peasantry from which they came.

This was the bottom of the food chain. From here, the more ambitious, hardworking, thrifty, and dreamers of a better life clawed their way upward and saw a future that was brighter. Most knew that they could not get there in a single step and took hope that their sacrifices would lead to their children achieving some part of the American dream. For them, it was a price they were paying for a future that would be better. For many of the next generation, it would prove to be true.

Chapter 8
The Great Depression

Life at its best on the plateau was a barely adequate existence for the vast majority of the people, but the hard-working immigrants were in a material utopia compared to the lives they had left behind in Eastern Europe and Ireland. However, even these seemingly good times were to come to an end.

The great depression descended like a cloud of doom on both the original settlers and the newcomers. No one was spared the abrupt decline in the demand for timber, coal, and firebrick. People with well-paying jobs were thrust into a present that was devastating and a foreseeable future that was bleak.

My first memories of the depression amount to seeing a great sadness and anxiety that covered the landscape. People seldom smiled and what little there was in the family was stretched to the breaking point.

Another memory I have is of sitting in a hot and dusty Model A Ford waiting while my father signed up for unemployment or some other benefit at the post office in the nearby town. I recall the sad expression on his face when he came to the car.

There was a lot of talk about Roosevelt saving the country. I have memories of the WPA and the CCC, which members of my family participated in. I can still visualize the local men and boys wearing goggles and swinging sledgehammers to crack rocks in a side road near the house. This was the first step in paving what was then known as a Pinchot road.

The complete length of the main old road that ran through the village was reworked with new hand laid stone culverts, and the side slopes were carefully graded with picks and shovels. The whole project employed a lot of people for a long time and provided hope in what was a society without a visible future.

The bank failures had happened in the years around my birth, but people still talked about the money they had lost and how you couldn't trust banks. This feeling was so deeply embedded that many of the adults carried this distrust for the rest of their lives.

My father was a life-long Republican, but he voted for Roosevelt all four times. His reasoning was that Roosevelt had saved the country. You can still stir up a discussion on this subject if you find someone old enough.

Humor tended to be of the gallows type. Herbert Hoover's promise of a chicken in every pot and a car in every garage was dusted off frequently, and people grimly chuckled when the overused punch line was given. "The chicken is in the pot because I can't afford to feed it, and the car is in the garage because I can't buy gasoline."

Another one you heard a lot is that pork might be a nickel a pound, but I don't have a nickel. Another more crude is that a whore not only had to do it for a nickel, but she had to swallow it. Of course, it was many years before I could figure this one out.

The Johnny Bulls on relief had little change in their lifestyle. However, they were now joined by hardworking people who felt ashamed that they had to take something for nothing. Human nature being what it is, desperation breeds strange bedfellows, and all managed to get along in their misery.

The old traditions of hand-me-down clothes now reached a new dimension. Not only were clothes handed down, but patched clothes were handed from child to child. Parts of worn-out clothes and shoes were used to repair other smaller items. I recall one of my older brothers cutting small shoe soles from worn out larger ones, straightening some old nails, and fixing a pair of shoes for me. It was the ultimate in recycling and reached a level that even today's treehuggers could not visualize.

Recycling covered everything conceivable. Absolutely nothing was thrown away. If it could not be used again, it was saved to sell to the "sheeny," who pushed a cart through the village calling, "Rags and old iron." The items sold didn't bring much, but any cash was welcome where there was none.

The immigrant men now had a lot of time on their hands, so they and the whole family tilled the soil in every conceivable place. Years later, when I saw the movie *Doctor Zhivago*, the scenes where Yuri and his family returned to the country after the revolution reminded me of the late 1930s and my childhood.

No smiles and maybe a bit of defiance. A long journey lies ahead for depression-era children.

The Irish and the eastern European peasants proved again that it was possible to live off the land, and although luxury was not in evidence, a reasonably healthy diet was the norm rather than the exception. The bounty of the summer—fruit, berries, beets, beans, and cucumbers—was canned for use in the winter months along with sauerkraut, cabbages, carrots, onions, and potatoes, so there was not a complete vitamin deficiency. Hogs, an occasional cow or calf, chickens, and wild game provided a supply of meat, so protein was available.

Those keeping cows had a reasonably steady supply of milk, so lack of calcium was not a problem. Usually, there was enough milk to sell it or give it to neighbors, the low price making both transactions nearly identical.

There was one enterprise that lasted beyond prohibition and its repeal in 1933, and that was the production of moonshine. The countryside was the natural place for this cottage industry, and those with the will and the means produced enough to bring in a little cash. Quality varied, but the demand was there even in hard times, and capitalism took its natural course.

Hobos were plentiful and smart enough to know that they could get a better meal in the countryside than they could in town. My mother apparently was known as a soft touch, because she invited them in and fed them whatever we had. We later suspected that they must have put some type of mark on the fence because they passed up a lot of places to come to our house. However, it may have been the presence of a barn, chicken coop, pigsty, and well-tended fields that provided the attraction.

They were invariably polite and grateful, and she always treated them with respect . . . except for one time, when she suggested that one should improve his life. He essentially told her to mind her own business, and she never did it again. It was a time that provided ample opportunities to live the teachings of Christ, for the least of His brethren were plentiful.

Sharing within a family was developed to an art form. For example, I recall about ten of us sharing an orange that we got on a special occasion. We not only divided it into sections, but we split each section so that each would have a share.

The depression experience marked both young and old. I think that the older ones suffered the most because their memories were more vivid, and they developed habits of sacrifice and strength of character that would serve them well in World War II and beyond. The young experienced fears that they would carry for a long time, and only the passing of years would help erase them. It really was an experience that tried people's souls.

Photo circa 1936. Eight of the ten kids shown in the photo above next to our two-bedroom house. Sleeping took a lot of creativity and sharing. There were two double beds in each room. Father and Mother kept the baby in their bed until the next one was born or was put in an iron crib. The iron crib was kept downstairs in the kitchen. At night, baby was in their bed. The other bed in their room had the next three youngest. The other bedroom had two beds—one for the boys and one for the girls. So some slept at the top and some at the bottom, all crosswise so there was some kicking for space going on. Girls slept in the same manner.

Chapter 9
Social Customs and Religion

For both the original settlers and the new immigrants, religion and forms of worship were the primary basis of social customs and interactions. In our small village, the Johnny Bulls had prayer meetings and bible study held in someone's home. A few people, usually elderly women, evolved as leaders and were consulted in matters of spiritual guidance. They usually hosted the meetings, and their homes were the center of other non-religious activity.

From my observation, most of the non-sexual intercourse among this group amounted to neighborly conversation, a lot of which originated while people were walking along the road. However, sexual intercourse, which had no apparent moral constraints, made use of any available meeting place, including outbuildings and the vast expanse of the woods in warmer weather.

During the warm months, the front porch served as a place to break the ice and start a conversation. We had a large porch with a swing, and when people of any ethnic persuasion walked by, they would first glance at whoever was sitting there. The body language reaction of the occupants was a subtle signal to strike up a conversation or to walk by with a simple hello. If a conversation were to be initiated, it would frequently start with the question, "Do you think the rain will hurt the rhubarb?" The answer, if it was friendly, was an invitation to stop and talk, which could result in hours of chatter about anything.

During the summer months, there was a tradition of making a community fire on the vacant school lot across from our house. Someone would get it started by suggesting that we go to the woods to gather some dry wood. This was usually about the time the shadows lengthened in the valley and the fire site was shaded, but the mist had not yet started to form over the cultivated fields near the *crick*.

The fire site was carefully chosen to avoid the cow pies left by the animals that grazed on the lot in the daytime. The old piles were easy to spot because the vegetation was higher there and cows did not eat the grass fertilized by their droppings. The new ones lay close to the ground, were wet and runny, and could be disgusting if stepped in.

People slowly joined around the fire, and all ethnic

groups were welcome. Seating was usually so you could look away from the highway toward the stream in the valley. By some unwritten rule, nobody ever faced in another direction, unless it was to get out of the smoke.

Stories of the good old days were mixed with juicy gossip about whoever was not there. Quitting time was determined by when the wood ran out after it turned dark, and all dispersed to their houses. I suspect that what we did was similar to tribal behavior thousands of years ago and would have been an interesting subject for an anthropologist.

The Johnny Bulls did not go in for elaborate weddings, with a simple get together of the wedding party taking place in one of the homes after a visit to a justice of the peace. Marriage seemed to be of secondary importance. There was a lot of premarital activity, and if you heard about a young girl getting married, the first question was usually if it was to her baby's father. I knew of one girl who first got married to her third child's father.

Funeral wakes, always held in the family home, were usually austere, with nothing to drink or eat being the norm. Normally, the village elder held a brief service at the home, and the deceased was interred with a minimum of ceremony. My mother visited all the village wakes, and the Protestants apparently had no problem with her saying her Catholic prayers over the deceased.

When she entered a house, she was cordially greeted,

knelt, made the sign of the cross, and silently said her Catholic prayers in Polish, with a special selection for funerals. The Johnny Bulls accepted this without hostility. Maybe the time of grief and shared Christianity created a brief period where animosities were put aside, and the realization set in that all were equal in death.

In the nearby town, the existence of formal Protestant churches led to more organized interaction. Attendance at services, Sunday school, choirs, dinners, picnics, and formal weddings and funerals made for a greater sense of community among this group.

The newer Irish immigrants formed their own Catholic church and carried on the traditions that they brought with them from Ireland. Formal weddings and elaborate wakes were the norm, but my knowledge of them is minimal because we did not cross ethnic lines in this regard. The Irish did not mix much with the Slavs until after World War II, when people started to socialize more on the basis of shared interests than ethnicity.

The Polish population was the most numerous of the Slavic immigrants and established their own Roman Catholic Church. The Czechs, Slovaks, and Lithuanians joined them, but it was always referred to as the Polish church.

The weddings, christenings, first communions, confirmations, and funerals, in conjunction with regular attendance at mass, formed the primary stimulus for interaction of this group.

The Russian and Ukrainians founded an Eastern Orthodox parish, with a building that had a copper onion dome. The different calendar for Christmas and Easter was always a point of discussion around town. They had an active social life centered around the church, but again, I have little knowledge of it because of ethnic isolation.

There was ethnic division in where the cemeteries were located. The original settlers and their offspring, all Protestants, had a burial ground just outside of one end of town. The Irish, Poles and other members of their church, and the Eastern Orthodox had a cluster of three separate cemeteries near the Orthodox building, commonly called the Russian church.

Going to mass at my church had its own rules. The women usually went inside to pray, while the men and older boys stayed outside and talked until the bell rang. They were always on time because one of them was the bell ringer. It was a rite of passage for a boy to stop going inside with his mother and stay outside to talk.

On the inside, small children of both sexes sat with their mothers on the female side of the aisle. The men and older boys sat on the other side. This custom persisted until after World War II, when some of the younger couples started sitting together. The older ones slowly changed and seating became a family affair. This was yet another example of the power of hormones and a nagging wife.

After this change, an old timer who only attended at Christmas midnight mass walked in after spending most of the evening drinking at the American Legion. He loudly proclaimed, "What is going on here, the men and women are all mixed up instead of sitting on their own sides." He quieted down after someone told him that things have changed but caused quite a stir initially.

The church held a picnic once a year, usually in a wooded location like a hunting camp. Food and drink were plentiful, with kegs of beer for the grownups and soft drinks for the younger set. Music was provided by an accordionist, and people danced.

Some of us were too young to really enjoy the festivities for a long time, and after eating and drinking our fill, were ready to go home. However, the mellow grownups were just hitting their stride. I once approached my father and said I was ready to go home. He replied that I should stay and listen to the music. My response went down in history and was quoted in my family for years later. I said, "I have a belly full of music." This expression was used frequently whenever music got monotonous, or the kind was not what a person enjoyed.

At one of the picnics, I first met a deaf-mute boy. His parents never brought him to church, and he did not receive the sacraments. Most of us didn't know he existed until we saw him at the picnic. He was quite a bit older than I, so I just watched and noted that his family and others he knew communicated well using sign language. I was saddened at the hardship that his family apparently had for years, for this was a time when the handicapped were not part of the open culture.

We had all read about Helen Keller, but this boy did not have the privilege of specialized schooling, and his life was different. However, it was apparent that he was loved and was capable of reciprocating in kind.

Christenings were somewhat low-key social affairs centered around the child's parents and the families of the Godparents. Typically, this would not exceed thirty people, if you counted all the older children. The baptism at the church was followed by a dinner and drinks at the home of the parents.

Depending upon finances, the party could be simple or more elaborate. Ethnic food was the norm, and could include golumki, pierogi, kielbasa, and roasted chicken. The older people always ate first, and the children followed, sometimes at a cluttered table that was unappetizing. The few christenings that I remember as a child were not fun events. We had none in my home that I remember, because I was the second-from-last child in our family.

A first communion was a major event in a family. It was preceded by a long period of study with frequent quizzes by the priest. My mother always took it seriously, and we kids always had all our prayers learned in Polish before we started the formal study.

She accomplished this by having us kneel in the kitchen before breakfast and before going to bed, and we started with the Our Father. When this was mastered, we learned the Hail Mary, Apostles Creed, Ten Commandments, and Seven Capital Sins. The concept of reciting these before breakfast was an incentive to learn, because when you did them well, you could eat. They were said out loud until you made your communion, at which time you could say them silently. When I started formal study, I learned the prayers in English, usually taught by one of my older sisters.

A first communion day was a big event at church, but not much of a social affair at home. The most elaborate it could get was to have a newly killed chicken for Sunday dinner, but the youngster was always made to feel special.

Christmas and Easter at our house were typical Polish events described well elsewhere. I remember Christmas as a time when we had roasted chicken after returning home after midnight mass because December 24th was a day of abstaining from meat.

Presents were rare at our house because of the large family and lack of money. After the older children started to work, they introduced what was an American custom, and we started getting individual presents.

Easter was a time of severe fasting on Good Friday, with the only meal being a soup made of potatoes and onions creamed with milk. The following Saturday was a time of taking food to church for blessing, and I remember the strong garlic smell from the different types of kielbasa.

Easter Monday included a custom we called dingus, where each family member poured cold water on the others when they were not expecting it. To get someone while in bed asleep was a real case of one-upmanship.

Polish weddings are known all over the world for being a real bash, and this is accurate. There is some truth to the expression that there is more fun at a Polish wedding than a WASP experiences in a lifetime. This may be an overstatement, but does describe the differences between the cultures.

The typical wedding starts about two days before the church ceremony, and the bride's home is the focal point for eating, drinking, and dancing to the point of near exhaustion. All people from out of town sleep in the house anywhere they can, and it is possible to fit 40 or 50 people into a three-bedroom house.

When they awake the next morning, the day is started with an eye opener, and the whole thing starts again. By the day of the wedding, everyone is happy to have a brief time of rest at the ceremony, and then the real party starts.

At this time, the invited guests join the family members, and the party really gets going. Everyone joins in helping with food and drinks, dish washing, dancing, and toasting the bride. After the cake cutting, the bride and groom depart in an appropriately decorated car, and the rest of the people party on until they collapse from exhaustion.

Drinks never run out at a good wedding, and the next day various people stop by to repair any personal bodily damage the may have sustained from drinking. This day, usually a Sunday, is the last day of the event, which most people welcome because their bodies could not take any more.

Funerals are initially a sad time, but by the time of the wake, held in the family home, they turn into subdued social events. It is considered good form to offer the visitors a drink and something to eat, but conversation is the only form of entertainment.

Two kinds of people attend a wake: the ones who drop in briefly, and the ones who stay. A priest usually makes a call later in the evening, and the rosary is recited. I can't recall any Polish wake that rivaled the often-discussed Irish type.

The priests we had came in many forms. Later in life I would hear them categorized as holy men and the others. I don't recall any holy men in our church during my childhood, but we had some of the others.

The first one I remember was a kind old man who presided at my first communion. He was always well-mannered and only occasionally gave a loud sermon.

He came to our house sometimes to share a few drinks with my father. His driver stayed outside in the car while he came inside with a pint of whiskey. As they drank, he would tell stories and we kids would listen intently. After they thought we were asleep, the stories got more personal, and once he got tearful and said that he never really wanted to be a priest but did it only because his mother wanted it.

His replacement was a horse of a different color, who had ambitions to rise in the church hierarchy. He projected an air of superiority and generally talked down to the people. Even at a young age, I knew that saving souls was not foremost on his agenda.

The legacy that he left in the town was to father a child with an unmarried girl. This apparently happened while he projected an image of morality and lectured the parish on the sin inherent in sexual promiscuity and adultery.

When my mother found out about this years later, she could not believe it. All her life she had been taught to respect priests and was surprised when I told her that I always thought he was an evil person.

All during my younger years, she referred to me as The Judge of Justice because I would point out who might be at fault in family disputes, even when she and my father got in arguments. She never held it against me, nor did he.

She once used this term when introducing me during the priest's annual census visit, and the priest looked at me sort of funny like maybe I could see through him. He quickly changed the subject, and I was convinced my assessment was correct.

In addition to churches, benevolent and social clubs added to the social mix. The Irish founded the local Knights of Columbus chapter and the Poles established the Saints Peter and Paul Society, both of which had religious origins but were primarily social in nature. The Polish organization had its own building, which was commonly called the Polish Hall. These groups were benevolent in nature because all were assessed a payment when a member died, the sum being passed on to the deceased's survivors.

These groups also did community service projects and held a candy distribution event with a Santa Claus at Christmas. I recall going to one with an older brother when I was about five years old, and he insisted that Santa was real. I spoiled his fun when I asked, "If Santa is real, why is he wearing the same belt that old man Gruda had on when we came in here a while ago?" Some kids really know how to spoil a good time.

My father was frequently an officer in the Saints Peter and Paul society, and when he was Secretary, he kept the meeting minutes in Polish. I would translate them to English for him and was always amused at the last entry where a motion was made, seconded, and unanimously approved to give 50 cents worth of free drinks to everyone attending the meeting. This was at a time when beer was 15 cents a bottle at the bar and a shot of whiskey was 25 cents.

The bylaws of the organization were amended in the late 1930s so that membership was open to all religions and ethnic groups except Jews, which maintained the Christian nature of the society. This was the Slavs' way of sending a subtle message that they were more tolerant than the other groups. The protestant businessmen quickly joined because the personal interaction stimulated sales. Each proposed member was voted on using a white and black ball system, with three black balls being required to turn down a prospect.

The Slovaks and Lithuanians, while attending the Polish church, maintained their ethnic identity by establishing their own benevolent societies, which were housed in separate facilities. They had the same broad membership rules as the Poles. The eastern orthodox people did not have a benevolent organization, but to some extent made use of the others.

There was a Masonic lodge in town, as well as chapters of the Elks and Moose, the latter being primarily protestant until ethnic barriers were broken down after World War II. In addition, there were commercial bars and dance halls throughout the town and in the small villages. A common observation was that there were more bars than churches in town.

The ethnic clubs did a good business because they had the advantage of being open on Sunday, when the commercial establishments were closed because of blue laws. An American Legion started after World War I, and it qualified as a private club that was not restricted by blue laws.

School functions like plays were multi-ethnic, but the Slav kids had minor roles, if any, until after World War II. However, the parents attended and got some exposure to what went on in the school. If there was a PTA, I was unaware of it.

Each year near the Fourth of July, a fireman's fair was held in the town. This attracted all the kids and quite a few grownups. The highlight on July 4th was a parade, usually consisting of fire trucks from nearby towns, new cars driven by various dealers, the high school band, the American Legion drill team, marching groups from the various benevolent societies, and anyone else who wanted to enter.

A roaming contract carnival was set up in the town

park for the fair, and the rubes were exposed to all kinds of entertainment to part them from their hard-earned cash. I started going to these at an early age, and my mother would usually give me a dime. I recall wandering around for a long time, trying to make up my mind where to spend it. I usually got a nickel box of crackerjack at the fair and bought an ice cream cone at a small store on the way home. The store was run by a kindhearted Irish family who practiced the teachings of Christ. One of the older kids we knew from school was the owner's son, and he always gave us a really nice scoop for a nickel.

Once when I was wandering around the fair, a few black kids from the brickyard were talking about how much money they had left, and the one with the least had five nickels. Compared to me, he was rich, but not the least bit of envy was in my heart.

A high wire trapeze act was usually part of the fair, and we all watched with fascination. For a couple of years, there was an act where a guy jumped off a tall tower into a tank of water covered with flaming gasoline. I watched this a lot of times and analyzed the physics of how he rotated and entered the water feet first, with the splash putting out nearly all of the fire before he came to the surface.

Speaking of rubes, this is where I first got taken. I was wandering around when I came to a tent where one of the female trapeze artists was sitting outside. She asked me to go down to the fire hall to get her a bucket of water. I did so out of kindness, with the possibility that she might pay me at least a nickel for doing the chore.

I brought her the bucket of water, and she thanked me but said to come back later and she would buy me a ride on the Ferris wheel. This was my first exposure to the check is in the mail syndrome, or a bird in the hand is better than a promise. I guess the carny mentality was so ingrained in her that she felt she had to con a kid. I was all of about ten years old at the time and was so kind-hearted that if she had asked, I would have done it for nothing.

The carny games were something to watch. You could tell that all were set up to almost win a prize, but even the winners got less than they expected. Much as the he-men would try to pound a mallet into a platform to get a little weight to ring a bell at the top of a mast, it always wound up not getting quite to the top. Most of the guys trying were the strong burly coal miner types who could work hard all day.

Depending upon the schedule, it was permissible for the carnival to be open on Sunday, but it was generally a day of rest in the region. All businesses except gas stations were closed. As children, we didn't mind this strict religious observation. It got us out of hard farm work except for taking care of the animals. It was a time to explore the woods and play the games that kids play.

Neighborhood kids played together regardless of ethnicity. Later in life, I would learn that animosities and bigotry had to be taught, and the young innocents had no predisposition to that type of behavior. Occasionally, during a childish spat, some slurs were exchanged but usually not taken seriously.

Somehow I got the function of assigning nicknames. Maybe it was because I read a lot and was more creative. Anyway, I nicknamed one kid with a nickname containing a vulgar word, and the name slowly got shortened to a single crude word. Of all my creations, this is one that I sincerely regret, but I had no malice in mind when I did it.

While the kids played together, we did not go into others homes nor did they enter ours. This was some boundary that was not crossed, although the reasons were never stated. Maybe it was an expression of being tolerant to a degree, but stopping short of complete acceptance.

We learned quite a bit about our Johnny Bull friends' families just by talking to the kids. Little bits and pieces of their conversations would fit into a pattern, and it was possible to tell who the real father of a specific child might be. When you added apparent physical properties, you could form some conclusions.

This ethnic group seemed to have few moral constraints on sexual activity, and a legal parent appeared to have no visible problem accepting a child fathered by some else. On one occasion, the jilted lover father went into a jealous rage when he was cut off, and shot his lover to death near our house.

The Slavs had similar problems, but not to the same degree. One jealous husband did his wife in with an ax while she was milking a cow, but I don't know if this had a deterrent effect on the rest of the population. Maybe the fact that there were no more cases attests to the effectiveness of the extreme measure.

Standing around the swimming pool fire in August

There was a community swimming hole about two miles from home. It was a dammed up trout stream that was spring fed from snow melt, and it was cold enough to give you goose bumps and shrivel your privates. An unwritten rule was that the first arrivals on a day would build a fire, even on a hot August day. The ritual then was to take a dip and stand around the fire.

When you stood near the fire with a chilled body, you sometimes got a pattern in your legs where the veins were visible. Someone named this condition fire pox, and it apparently was passed down from earlier generations.

The only membership requirement was that you had to help repair the stone dam each year after the spring floods. This was done by restacking the rocks and stuffing the seams with clumps of swamp grass. The whole process resembled a bunch of beavers at work.

The rock-walled swimming hole

The first arrivals also had to chase the snakes away from the dam and grassy area. We killed every snake that we could, but most would slither between the rocks or occasionally into the sandy bottom of the pool. We noted where they went and avoided that part.

One day we had killed a snake, and the conversation took on a Tom Sawyer slant about when snakes actually die. Nearly everyone believed the myth that they lived until sunset, so I picked up the snake and pitched it into the fire, where we watched it burn to ashes.

I asked the other kids if it was dead, and they quickly responded that it was not dead until the ashes cooled. Who said that you could ever get ahead of an Appalachian mountain kid when it came to a good legend?

Fear of snakes was taught to us at an early age. One day a friend and I were walking home from fishing and a rattlesnake was crawling slowly across the road ahead of us. My friend immediately said, "I get the rattles," and I didn't argue.

We slowly approached the snake and tried to kill it with large rocks. However, we were so cautious that we didn't come anywhere near killing it, and it crawled into some brush and ferns where we did not care to pursue. Neither of us regretted not getting it, and it was just a good story to tell.

In the village, there was a great tendency to mind other people's business. This was sometimes subtle but frequently blatant like sitting at a window and looking out for hours like some self-appointed watchman. Our idle neighbor Doc was king of this activity, or inactivity if you wish. He missed nothing.

A female neighbor about two houses away was no

slouch at watching. If you talked to her, she would ask who you had visiting and had a count of all people, their sexes, and general appearance. My mother did some of the same with her and once got so curious that she sent me to ask about some duck eggs so I could find out who was visiting.

These women had an unofficial contest about who hung up the first piece of wash on Monday, and my mother usually won because she just rinsed an old cellar rug before she got her full wash going. The other woman never did catch on to this trick.

The interaction of religion and social customs persisted until the mid-20th century, when the older generation started dying off, the younger ones moved away, and ethnic identities became secondary. The change was accelerated when coal and railroads declined, and the village lost nearly 80 percent of its population. The onset of the television age also had an influence.

Looking back from the beginning of the 21st century, the soil is not farmed and the cows no longer roam the woods. Evergreens have taken over the fence rows and obscured the view of neighbors. Wakes are held in the funeral home, and the front porches have disappeared or been turned into extra rooms. People seldom walk along the road, and the old swimming hole is silted full. The dead snake that was thrown into the fire got its sunset, and a whole lot of other things did too.

In the nearby town, the Polish Hall lost its ethnic identity and religious affiliation. It ran as a social club for a while but eventually folded and was sold to the Loyal Order of the Moose. Ever vigilant for humor, the locals began calling it the Mooski.

The Polish church suffered a more tragic fate, and was consolidated with the Irish parish. To add insult to injury, the building that had been constructed with the sacrifices of immigrant coal miners was torn down, despite passionate pleas to the bishop to preserve it as a historical site. The lot now has a garage used by the house next door.

When it was closed, my father quit going to church. After a few months, he was visited by the Irish pastor who asked why he was not attending mass. My father replied that his church had been torn down. The pastor responded that God would punish those who did not attend mass. My father countered that He would also punish those who tore down houses of God.

The pastor, who was an alcoholic, died a tragic death from exposure when he fell into a strip mine hole while he was drunk. The circumstances were a symbolic end to a sordid chapter in the way the bishop treated people of deep faith. The church cemetery is still there under the original name, so at least the dead were allowed to rest in peace. The names on the gravestones and the memories of their descendants are the only testimonial to their faith and sacrifice.

Chapter 10
Figures of Speech

American speech is littered with expressions that have roots in real-life activities of colonial America. Terms like "keep your powder dry," a "flash in the pan," "going off half-cocked," and "the whole thing, lock, stock, and barrel" are directly related to use of flintlock muzzle loading firearms. These expressions have endured even though the activity has not.

On the Allegheny Plateau, similarly derived expressions were based on real-life activities of the people in the villages and farms near the small towns. The expression "A long row to hoe" and "A hard row to hoe" or the extremely difficult "Long hard row to hoe" were real to the men and boys, and occasionally women, who hoed rows of corn, beans, and potatoes in plots that were sometimes freshly turned sod.

Perseverance and self discipline were required to

tackle a long or hard, or both, row, when you knew that getting to the end meant that another was waiting for you. A backbreaking day at this activity really built character that carried over to other endeavors.

Making hay while the sun shines was also real. The first settlers, and later the eastern European immigrants, mowed hay with a scythe, like that carried by the grim reaper, and dried it in the fields. It was raked by hand and stored in a barn loft or in a haystack. About four consecutive days of sunshine were required for a good crop to be harvested.

Waiting until the cows came home was real, because the cows were let loose to graze in the nearby woods. Also, having the chickens come home to roost was a daily event when the chickens were allowed to range freely.

A late spring snow was called an onion snow because it frequently fell on a garden where newly sprouted onions had appeared. For those who had seen snow lying on onion shoots, it was an imaginative and vivid description.

Speech patterns in general were interesting on the plateau. The original settlers and their descendants spoke a dialect that evolved from their colonial English. Terms like "commence" instead of "begin" were common, and "agin we get there" was used instead of "until we get there."

If you asked any of these natives if they spoke with

an accent, they would deny it, but the Pennsylvania Appalachian lilting pattern was popular. The term "Ah" instead of "I" was used, as in "Ah'll do it" instead of "I'll do it." The word fish was pronounced as "feesh," eagle was "iggle," and steel was "still" as in "still mill" or "Pittsburgh Stillers."

Questions had some interesting forms. They could take the style of "That's right, hain't it?" or "We should go to town, huh, John?"

The accepted past tense of steal was "stold." Skint meant skinned, and "clean over there" was preferred over "clear over there." The term "youse" was looked down upon as a big city expression. The locals proudly substituted "younze" for it and felt superior to the occasional visitor from the city.

Some valid words were applied in a strange fashion. The noontime meal was called dinner, and a miner carried a dinner bucket to work for his midday nourishment. The evening meal was called supper and was eaten at "supper time" which was no later than 5:00PM.

The term living room was unheard of, and the space was simply called the "room." Outhouses were common but were called "the shit house" or "the toilet." To straighten up a messy room was to "red it up" which may have come from making it ready for visitors.

An opportunity to "zing" someone in speech was seldom passed up. If a local got a new red pickup truck and proudly showed it to a neighbor, he was likely to get a response such as "You shoulda got a redder one," or "It's a nice truck, but I wouldn't own a Shivvy," if the truck happened to be a Chevrolet.

If a neighbor happened to stop to talk while someone was working, it was not long before the visitor would critique the job and say, "Where you made your mistake is . . ." One-upmanship was a sport that everyone played. Any opening was normally met with a verbal uppercut to the jaw.

A well-worn story involved two immigrants who were walking home after drinking a few at a local ethnic club. One considered himself to be the worlds greatest gift to women and took every opportunity to brag about it. The other was the father of sixteen children and believed in letting actions speak louder than words.

The story has it that the two came to a bridge over a small stream and took the opportunity to drain their bodies of some of the liquid that had been so liberally input. After a few moments of urinating, the braggart said, "The water is cold, huh?" The prolific father answered, "Not very deep, though."

The Irish immigrants introduced terms like "blarney and leprechauns," but they did not have a great influence in changing the embedded patterns, apparently because their English was close to that spoken by the natives.

The eastern Europeans brought with them the Slavic

languages that were a crude peasant form of the mother tongues. These rapidly became corrupted with English and modified English words that they adopted, usually because they had no Slavic equivalent.

For example, most left the old country when it was still in the horse and buggy period. Therefore, they called a car a "cara" because they had never known the word "samohod." Similarly, they had lived in single-floored cottages, so they called stair steps "shtepsi."

Other words were modified for easier pronunciation such as "grach" for garage, "villbara" for wheelbarrow, "frontovi porch" for front porch, "bara" for bar, "screwdriverr" for screwdriver, "jara" for jar, "barna" for barn, "lampa" for lamp, "grapse" for grape, "mulak" for mule, "trock" for truck, etc.

Some words were adopted directly because they needed no pronunciation help. The common terms such as wrench, pick, pigpen, and radio were used without modification.

The resulting language was something that their relatives in the old country would have had a hard time comprehending if they had heard it.

The immigrants' children wound up speaking a better brand of English than the natives. They were not exposed to the archaic forms at home, and usually spoke their parent's Slavic language. Their English was closer to the type taught in school, although some of the less qualified teachers had localisms in their speech.

One teacher with minimal science training pronounced inertia as "in-ear-ee-ya." Another who taught history related the story of the Boston "mass-ah-cree." This led to some interesting political choices when the students would recite their lessons back to the teachers.

The children of the immigrants, with their better brand of English, had more influence in changing local speech patterns than the descendants of the original settlers, primarily because they were greater in numbers as a result of the larger immigrant families. Also, for the most part, their bilingualism made further study of foreign languages easier, and they excelled at high school Latin and French.

Sometimes expressions came from humorous events that were so vivid they became everlasting. One such resulted from an incident at a wake held in a home, as was the custom at the time.

It was considered good manners to serve something to eat about midway through the evening hours of a wake, and one housewife prepared a large serving bowl of noodles, known as kluskis, mixed with cottage cheese and bacon bits. She set it in the middle of the table with a large spoon.

When she went to get some smaller plates, a local named Gus pulled the whole bowl to his seat and began to eat it with the serving spoon. Everyone stared in amazement, but most saw the humor in the event.

As the story got told later, the expression "being like Gus and the kluskis" got to be standard usage whenever anyone took an unusually large helping from a serving dish. It endures in my home to this day.

Chapter 11
The Village Store

When the immigrants settled in my village, none had automobiles, and they walked to the nearby town to shop for groceries. They were usually taken advantage of by the Johnny Bull merchants and given inferior cuts of meat and sometimes made to wait while the grocer served an old customer who arrived later.

This treatment led to a few more enterprising immigrants starting small stores of their own. We had one such establishment in the middle of our village. It stocked nearly all the basics but only had meat in cooler weather when some local butchering took place. A regular supply of meat could be obtained from an immigrant store in the nearby town.

The store in our village had a smell typical of goods stored in barrels and bins. It had canned goods, candy, chewing tobacco, roll your own tobacco and papers, bakery bread, and mining supplies such as carbide and black powder, which was stored outside of the building. Kerosene for lamps was also stocked and kept in a drum behind the store.

To keep some of the goods from freezing, a parlor-type stove was in the building, but it had a fire only in cold weather. It contributed to the overall ambience.

The people who ran the store also farmed a fair-sized piece of land, so they did not have a full-time clerk in the store. If customers wanted something, they would go to the back of the store porch and yell, "In the store." This would usually bring the proprietor, his wife, or one of the children to open the store and serve the customer.

The village store did not extend credit, and anyone who wanted to "charge" a purchase needed to do so with one of the town merchants. I recall stopping at a market on the way home from high school with a pal, and he bought two pounds of neck bones and charged it to his father's account.

In a neighboring village, one of the stores ran a small tavern along with the usual stock. This attracted a different clientele in the evening, and a jovial atmosphere prevailed.

The tavern owner took pride in running a friendly place to cultivate business and tolerated a lot from the patrons. One evening his patience was tested to an extreme, when an intoxicated neighbor decided to play a practical joke when he departed by shitting in the seat of a horse-drawn wagon that the owner had parked outside.

When the owner saw the shit the next morning, he came up with an expression that became part of local lore. He said, "Business is business, but shit in the wagon is not business."

Not long after World War II ended, the village stores and taverns slowly died out, supermarkets with pre-wrapped meat opened, and a way of life disappeared.

Chapter 12
The Kitchen Stove

When primitive man first discovered fire, the warmth and light of the flames quickly became the center of family activity, especially after dark. A simple fire likely evolved into a ring of stones, which further developed into a pile of stones, which was the forerunner to the fireplace.

In colonial America, the fireplace was a focal point of life, especially in the winter. John Greenleaf Whittier, in the poem *Snowbound* describes this exquisitely.

It took a long time for a metal stove to replace the fireplace as a primary source of heat and as a means of cooking, apparently because of the difficulty in producing abundant and cheap metal.

In our village, the simple houses had a wood and coal-burning stove in the kitchen. This was the primary means of cooking and sometimes the only source of heat in winter. The more affluent homes had a wood and coal parlor stove, but central heating with a furnace was unknown. In extreme cold, the oven door was kept open to increase the flow of heat.

Because of the stove, the kitchen became the gathering place for the family. It was only after the advent of radio, which most considered to be a prestige acquisition, that the parlor, or *room*, attracted some of the family members from the kitchen.

In our house, the kitchen was the place for learning prayers, telling stories, stripping chicken and duck feathers for pillows and pierzyni, and shelling beans and peas. This was also where food and drinks were served to visitors. Most meals were eaten at a kitchen table, with the dining room used only for Sunday dinner and special occasions such as Christmas.

The stoves were a prized item and came in many brands. The one that is still in our house in the village was bought new in 1940 and serves as a focal point for the family which now includes great grandchildren of my parents.

Using a stove like this is an art form. First, patience is required to start a fire and get the massive iron top up to cooking temperature. A fire is laid using crumpled newspaper followed by twigs and topped with some small dry wood. After making sure the lower air vent is open and the oven diverter is in a position for the draft to go straight to the flue pipe, the paper is ignited.

As the fire builds, more wood is added until the box is full. When the fire is going well, the oven diverter is closed so that the top of the stove heats up uniformly. After about 15 minutes you are ready for cooking.

The stove as seen today

A stove like this makes frying bacon a mouth-watering experience. As the bacon cooks, a bit of it splatters out of the frying pan and is vaporized on the hot stove top. This distributes an aroma that wafts throughout the whole house, making sound sleepers rise and anticipate breakfast.

We had none during my childhood, but doing steaks now in a large cast iron frying pan provides a similar experience. The sizzling fat also splatters on the stovetop and makes the meal something to anticipate. There is a lot to be said for a more primitive way of food preparation.

There is one major downside to this type of cooking, and that is summer heat. All windows and doors need to be open for ventilation, and the heat is still oppressive. On the occasions when vegetables, fruits, and berries were canned in mason jars, the fire needed to be hot for most of the day. This is likely what led to the expression about slaving over a hot stove all day.

A few of the houses had what was called a summer kitchen. This was a small building behind the main house, where the stove heat did not bother the house occupants. Food prepared here was brought into the house kitchen or dining room. In later years, I saw something similar at the Mount Vernon mansion, where no cooking was done inside the main quarters.

Chapter 13
Tilling the Soil

If an observer looking down from the sky could simultaneously observe the farming methods used by the eastern European peasants and their offspring in central Pennsylvania, he would see little difference. In both cases the human body and hand tools coaxed the bounty from the land. Every living thing was treated with a care that bordered on worship, for the very survival of mankind depended upon the yield of small parcels of land.

The lessons that the immigrants learned in the old country served them well during the great depression. They seldom went hungry, and although not eating in luxury, they had the basics that they and their children produced themselves. Every usable piece of land was cultivated.

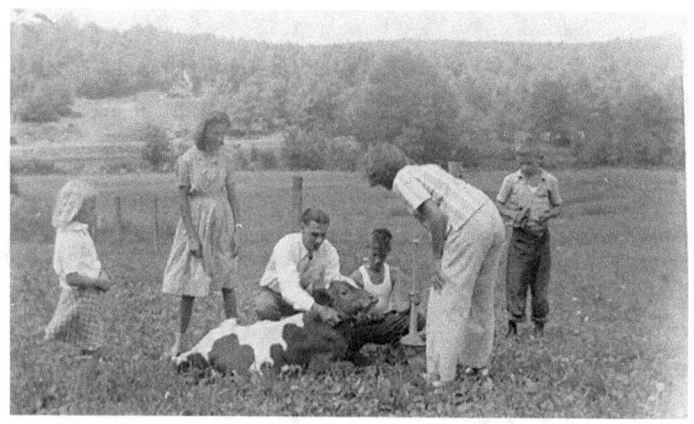

Every bit of land was used for something.

Food came at a great price paid in backbreaking labor. Everything produced in the gardens, including onions, carrots, radishes, beets, lettuce, peas, garlic, cucumbers, pumpkins, tomatoes, cabbages, cauliflowers, and beans required a lot of hard work. First the soil was spaded, then broken up and raked, and seeds were planted in neat rows.

Weeding came next, and there were a lot of weeds because of the cow manure used for fertilizer. I recall that weed pulling was my transition from childhood play to useful work. When I was about four or five, my mother showed me how to carefully remove weeds from a row of emerging plants, and I plucked them from the soil with my tiny hands. It was meticulous toil, but I worked at it until my assignment was done.

Little did I realize the power that I had over the weeds, for I had full control over their destiny as to which one lived or died. Conversely, they had a part in shaping my character and future, for the discipline I learned would be with me forever.

Next came careful cultivating with a hoe, and more weed pulling. Weeding and cultivating were repeated until the plants became large enough to fill the spaces between rows.

Frugality prevailed even in this process. The weeds that were pulled were fed to the chickens that were cooped so that they would not destroy the gardens.

Feeding chickens in a wire pen

The larger potato and corn fields were worked in a similar manner, except they were first plowed instead of spaded. Plowing was done for a small fee by a friendly neighbor with a horse, and the newly-turned soil was harrowed. My earliest memories of plowing are of a neighbor using a nervous horse that jerked a lot, and every time it did so, the farmer called the horse a "cock sucker." For an Appalachian youngster, vocabulary expanded at an early age.

Harvesting wheat like it was done centuries ago

The potato and cornfields were cultivated by hand with a hoe, and a long hard row to hoe had real meaning. There is probably no more backbreaking labor in the world than hoeing a field, and knowing that every time you finished a row, another was waiting for you. It may have built character, but the cost of the lessons was dear.

Hay was harvested just as it was in the old country peasant fields. It was cut by hand with a straight handled scythe similar to that seen in depictions of the grim reaper. Using a scythe involves a skill that is acquired but difficult to describe. After you swing and make a cut, you need to move slightly ahead so that your next swing takes uncut grass. The step is about two or three inches in length, and is done without thinking about it. When you are done with a row, you can look back and see two grooves in the sod where your feet had moved slowly.

Wheat was also harvested with a scythe and bundled into sheaves. Later the grains were separated with a flail, and the wind was used to separate the grain from the chaff.

Bundling wheat into sheaves

Hay was dried where it lay, and if the weather was sunny, a good crop was harvested. However, if it rained, the hay had to be carefully lifted and fluffed with a pitchfork so that the rainwater would dry out. If you got a few days of rain after cutting, the crop was usually ruined and became moldy. It was then used for bedding, for the cows even if hungry would not eat it.

The hay was stored in the barn or in a haystack if there was too much. A good crop smelled aromatic because of the variety of grasses, and the expression sweet smelling hay had real meaning.

Potato growing was a competitive art, and the person who got the biggest and most from a parcel was the winner whose only reward was bragging rights. Most people developed their own techniques and were stubborn in sticking with them.

The crop was subject to insects and various blights. Spraying the vines about twice during growing with a mixture of copper sulfate and lime dissolved in water made for a healthy crop.

Potatoes were harvested in September by digging them up carefully with a spade or hoe. They were dried of exterior moisture and then stored in a root cellar or dark corner of a house cellar. With care, they would last well into the beginning of the next summer.

My father was known as a good potato grower, but our mother and the kids did most of the backbreaking work. As always, humor worked its way into the situation. The story goes that someone once stopped and asked to buy a half bushel of potatoes, and my father refused him by saying that he would not cut one of his potatoes in half for anyone.

Throughout the summer, as the various crops were harvested, they were consumed, canned in mason jars, or stored. Cucumbers were pickled along with dill, and beans and beets were canned. A canned combination called "chow chow" included beans, onions, and small cauliflower bits. Corn was eaten off the cob as it ripened and pumpkins were made into pie or an old country creamed soup. Some cabbage was stored and then used by peeling off the dried leaves. Most was made into sauerkraut by shredding it into thin slices with a special cutter, and salting and stomping it into a large crock or barrel.

The best summer dish was a fresh soup, which included a bit of pork, carrots, yellow and green beans, new potatoes, and onions. The whole thing was creamed with fresh milk and a bit of browned flour.

Tomatoes were canned or made into ketchup, which had a flavor unlike the commercial variety. Mature onions and garlic were stored by hanging them in a dry place. Carrots were kept in a barrel filled with sand.

When you added the various fruits that were canned, and the milk and meat available most of the year, the total diet was reasonably healthy. Unfortunately, the residents of the nearby town did not enjoy the same.

The byproducts of all the cultivation and harvesting—and there were many including beet and carrot tops, peelings, corncobs, and leftovers—were fed to the hogs. In addition, a special crop of cow beets was grown especially for them. Sad to say, they ate better than a lot of people during the great depression but paid the price by themselves being consumed.

All of the hard work and patience involved in this method of farming bred a group of individuals where instant gratification was not part of their operating philosophy. When faced with any seemingly impossible task, an expression used by my father always comes to mind. When starting out on a large field of potatoes that needed hoeing, he would say, "The eyes are afraid, but the hands will do it."

Chapter 14
Butchering Time

With refrigeration being rare except in the grocery stores, killing farm animals for food was limited to chickens, ducks, and an occasional tame rabbit during the warm months from April through early November. This may have been the reason that chicken became a well-known Sunday dinner meal, because it was killed and eaten in the same day.

The cool weather of late fall and winter made it possible to preserve meat longer by storing it in an outbuilding like a barn or shed. Along about Thanksgiving Day, it became a village ritual to butcher hogs and old milk cows, and later in the day you could see them hanging from poles, trees, and tripod-like devices.

Hog butchering as I knew it was a fairly simple but labor-intensive project that took nearly all day for a single pig. One or more additional days were required to process the quartered meat into edible sausages, bacon, and cured hams.

There is an old saying that a well-butchered hog is completely used except for the squeal. This was almost true in our family, except that we did not use the hair or hooves.

The process started with heating about twenty gallons of water and sharpening knives. It helped to have at least two people to kill the pig, because the blood was saved, to later be used in a type of sausage.

The pig was stunned by shooting it between the eyes with a 22 caliber rifle. A skilled person then made a small hole in the center of the throat, much like a tracheotomy. When the knife was inserted, it was used to internally cut the throat veins and arteries and the blood was caught in a pot by a second person as it flowed from the small external hole. As the blood drained, the pig died.

Now the hard work began. The carcass was moved to the hair removal area, which usually consisted of a rough plank platform near the ground. In our family, burlap bags were laid on the carcass, and scalding hot water was poured on and allowed to set long enough to loosen the hair. The bags were removed, and a long sharp knife was used much like a razor to scrape off the hair. The process was repeated until the pig was bald.

The pig was next raised by a wooden cross pole inserted through holes cut in the first joint of the hind legs. Lifting was performed by brute force or with a block and tackle.

Residual fine hair was next scorched off with a blowtorch or pieces of flaming newspaper wrapped into tight cylinders. The idea was to get the skin completely free of hair.

Now a bit of specialty work was required. The anus was carefully separated from the surrounding tissue in such a way that it could be tightly tied to keep any fecal matter from contaminating the meat. This provided an occasion for a bit of humor, because the anus cutter was referred to as an asshole specialist.

The head was next removed by cutting around the neck with a sharp knife. If this was done in the proper place, the head could be separated by twisting it and no sawing was required.

An incision was now made along the belly from between the hind legs all the way thorough the breastbone to the remaining neck. The innards were then separated from the spine tissue and allowed to collect in a large washtub. If this process was done with skill and care, a completely clean and empty carcass resulted. It was now allowed to hang and cool.

Attention was now focused on the gut pile. The liver, lungs, heart, and kidneys were separated from the stomach and intestines. The bladder was carefully removed, flushed out, inflated, tied off, dried, and used as a child's toy.

Without going into disgusting detail, the stomach and intestines were separated and flushed out, to be used as sausage casings. The small intestines needed to be turned inside out and scraped to turn them into a clean thin sausage casing. This was another job that could be called character building. It took nerves of steel to stand the smell and visual effects.

When it came to eating the sausage later, it was necessary to put the whole matter out of your mind. There is a lot of truth to the expression that while sausage tastes good, you really don't want to see it being made. It is interesting to note that to this day, you can buy a hog stomach in a good Pennsylvania Dutch market for use in making a delicacy known as hog maw.

With the nasty work done, we were now entitled to rest, and in our house it was not usual to have any of the hog on the same day it was butchered. On some occasions, a bit of the easy-to-get-to neck meat was fried up, but we had been so busy butchering that there was no time for an elaborate meal.

At about sunset, and after the carcass had cooled, it was sawed vertically through the backbone and then each side was separated into front and hind quarters. These were hung indoors in the cool cellar to await the work of the next day.

With an early morning start, the meat was separated

into the parts to be cured and smoked, like bacon sides and hams. These were placed in a barrel of water containing salt and saltpeter. After a few months, they were smoked over coals of hickory or apple wood.

The rest was cut into edible parts like chops and that which would be ground into sausage. Every part was processed, including the head and feet. The hooves were loosened from the feet by temporarily heating them in the open flame of the kitchen stove.

A lot of anatomy was learned in cutting up a head. The eyes were particularly interesting, but they were discarded. All of the scrap meat from the head was combined with that of the feet and made into head cheese which was also called souse in some cultures. This was boiled and allowed to cool in shallow pans, where it jelled.

Two kinds of sausage were made. The first was made from ground meat, seasoned with black pepper, salt, saltpeter, and mustard seed, and stuffed into the casings made from the small intestines. It was allowed to cure in the low heat behind the kitchen stove, where it turned slightly red. It was stored in a cool place like the barn or attic, and would last a few months without refrigeration.

The quality of the sausage was determined by the selection of meat used. The ultimate was to use the whole hog to make sausage, including the hams and loins. This was the origin of the expression "going whole hog" when referring to something that was as good as you could get.

The second sausage was blood sausage, or kishka in the Slavic culture. The blood saved during killing was combined with all the ground organs and some low quality meat, buckwheat groats, and then boiled with seasoning consisting only of black pepper. After cooling, it was spooned into the stomach and large intestine and then gently simmered for about a half day. It was eaten either sliced or pan fried.

Old milk cows were butchered in a similar manner, except the hide was skinned off. The meat was processed into edible cuts and hamburger. Sausage was not made and the intestines, including the stomach, were buried in a handy place. Possibly, because there was so much to a cow, the dish known as tripe was not made in our family.

Because of the size of a cow, it was normal to sell quarters or cuts to neighbors. Sometimes paybacks were made in kind for something acquired from the butchering done by someone else. This was done with people you could trust, and I am not aware of any disputes.

Chapter 15
The Robins of My Youth

We had two cherry trees on the south side of the house. They were not the sweet black kind but were what is known as sour cherries. We ate the fruit when it became ripe, and sometimes our mother would use the cherries to make a pie.

The robins liked to build nests in the trees, and they also liked the fruit when it became ripe. In fact, it became a bit of a contest with the robins as to who could stand to eat the cherries when they were just ripening. If we humans waited for them to get good and sweet, the robins would get to them earlier and we would have none.

When I was about five, I noticed that a robin was building a nest in one of the trees. It was low enough that I could climb the tree and look into it. Everyone said that I should not do it, because the robin would abandon the nest if a human came near it.

I climbed and looked anyway and saw that the bird had laid some eggs in the nest. After I descended, the robin came back to the nest and sat on the eggs, so another myth was debunked. Perhaps I was so small and harmless looking that the mother made an exception in my case. I did not disturb the robin every day, but would occasionally look into the nest to see if the birds had hatched.

On one of my visits, I saw four newly hatched little robins. I made a chirping sound like the mother did, and they opened their mouths and held them up to receive food. It reminded me of people waiting to receive communion at mass.

On my next trip to the nest, I took some crushed cherries, and when I chirped, the robins opened their beaks, and I dropped some cherry into each. They swallowed it and waited for more.

As the robins grew, I helped the mother feed them and would occasionally give them bits of earthworm after the cherries were gone. They grew in size and developed feathers.

The robins grew to the extent that they crowded the nest. I noted that the mother always removed their droppings and kept the nest clean.

One day, I climbed the tree, and the robins were gone. I looked around for them and saw one fluttering on the ground at some distance from the tree, trying its wings.

I was a little sad that my robins had flown the nest, but I was happy that they had started lives of their own. I thought that one day I would do the same.

Chapter 16
The Great Strawberry Raid

We did not have anyone in the village who qualified as a *Tom Sawyer* or *Huckleberry Finn*. However, my ethnic Russian pal Ivan was the nearest to it, except he had a reputation for being meaner than snot. He was so mean that nobody even dared to give him a nickname.

He also had a cussing vocabulary that was unequaled, even by the grownups. When I first started hanging around with him, I used a few of his words at home, but was quickly told that they were not acceptable. In no time at all, I filtered them out, but they did become part of my adult vocabulary, especially in special circumstances.

He was a true adventurer and set a pace that we more disciplined kids were taught to avoid. Anything that was available became fair game for Ivan to steal, and we soon learned to not ask questions about where one of his new acquisitions came from.

We were accustomed to picking wild strawberries in the woods, and these were delicious but small and scarce. When their season had passed, Ivan one day mentioned that he knew where we could get some cultivated ones that would be ripe in about a week. He told us they were in a patch near one of the Negro shanties in the next village near the brick yard. He said they were across the road from the buildings and we would not be seen if we sneaked in from the woods.

Curiosity overcame my common sense, and I agreed to join him and a couple of other kids in visiting the patch. We planned it like a military raid.

The distance we needed to go was about three miles, and we first walked on the paved road. For the last mile, we left the road and made our way through the woods and a rhododendron thicket. For the last hundred yards, we crawled on our hands and knees to the edge of the patch.

Our intention the whole time was just to eat some strawberries, and we proceeded to do so. We let our guard down and picked with enthusiasm.

A slight noise alerted us, and we looked up to see what appeared to be a monstrous looking black man standing at the other end of the patch. From our perspective, he certainly looked like someone to be feared.

Everyone panicked and got up and ran like hell into

the woods and the rhododendron. We could hear a deep voice laughing behind us, and we didn't stop until we ran out of breath a few hundred yards later.

Needless to say, after that we avoided the village and the shanties for a long time. I personally chose not to take part in any of Ivan's adventures that even had a hint of larceny attached to them. However, we still explored the mines and woods, and did some things that Tom and Huck would have been proud of.

Chapter 17
Theft in the Village

The honesty of people in my village was governed by the ethics that each had developed as part of their upbringing and religious education. Some strictly adhered to the principle of *thou shall not steal,* and you soon learned to trust them.

Some thought that everything you could get your hands on was fair game. These were the ones that made people put locks on the chicken coops, carefully put tools away after a day's work, and lock the house doors when you went to bed.

One year we had an especially good crop of cabbages and looked forward to our traditional dish of stuffed cabbage along with putting some away in a crock as sauerkraut. After getting up one morning and going to the garden to take a look, we quickly noted that all the cabbages were gone. They had been cleanly cut off the roots so that only the usable heads were gone.

This was a disappointment but not something that came as a surprise. We still had our stuffed cabbages and kraut, but it required buying some from a neighbor who had not suffered theft.

In the time before I was old enough to personally see it, there was a practice of farmers from over the mountain bringing wagonloads of goods through our village to be sold in the nearby town. The rough village teens looked upon this as an opportunity to get some free stuff, so they would wait near a curve where the horses and wagon would be going slow and then jump up on the wagon. Then would then throw goods from the wagon.

The farmer was usually alone, so he had little choice in defending himself from the thugs. Usually he would whip the horses into a run to get out of the village. Later, the experienced wagon drivers would whip the horses into a run before the entrance to the village, and go like hell until coming out the other side.

Picking loose coal from the railroad tracks was considered to be acceptable behavior, and many people did it. However, some creative thieves wanted to make it easier. One in particular would hop on a coal car that was moving slowly up the double track grade. He would then make a stack of coal lumps on the edge of the car, and when getting near his house, push the whole load off.

During the depression, all scrap iron was scavenged

from the old mines and sold to peddlers. Initially, this included old railroad track spikes, plates, and bits of rail. However, this soon got out of hand and some operating tracks became fair game for theft. This was stopped when the peddlers refused to take railroad iron because they could not resell it without being accused of accepting stolen goods.

Once we had a caravan of gypsies camp in a field across the creek from our house. We looked upon them with interest because it was something new to us. We noticed how quickly they unpacked tents from their old cars and started cook fires. We kept our distance and looked upon them with suspicion. They packed up and left the next morning.

It was summer time, so a bit later my pal Ivan came over to our place. The first words out of his mouth were "Those goddam gypsies not only sneaked into our barn and milked the cow last night, they even stolt the fucking bucket." It was a bit humorous that our village master thief had been one-upped by the gypsies.

We had enough honest people in the village that we could tolerate and avoid the bad seeds, so theft did not have a serious impact on our lives. It was just another lesson that there is no surprise or shock in how some people behave, just a lot of disappointment.

Chapter 18
Horse Theft

There were a few plow horses in our village and in the nearby countryside. They were well cared for and earned their keep by working the fields not only for their owners but also for neighbors. A part of the owner's farm was usually set aside as pasture for these beasts.

An occasional attempt to let a horse run free with the cows usually met with tragedy. I recall being awakened one night by a gunshot. It seems that a free running horse had been struck by a car and suffered a broken leg.

With the owner's permission, a neighbor had shot the horse between the eyes. I recall the neat hole and the dead horse by the side of the road.

Later in the day, a truck arrived from over the mountain and took the carcass away. I was told that the hide would go to a tannery and the rest of the horse would be used for dog food and other products. In later years, I would learn that Jell-O was one of the byproducts.

The coalmines had a lot of ponies and mules that spent their working time in the mines. They were kept in a mule barn that sometimes had a small fenced outdoor area for them to get some sunlight and roll in the dirt. This was not large enough to grow grass, so all feeding was done with hay and oats that was hauled to the mine.

Boys being what they were, there was a great temptation to ride both the farm horses and the mine mules and ponies. Sometimes the owners let the boys ride to exercise the animals when they were not being used for a long time. My pal Ivan had a brother who was talented at riding, and a neighbor let him ride a pony. He took to it like a Mongol from the steppes, and would give us a bareback demonstration that was good enough to star as an Indian in a western movie.

The working mules kept at the mines were a different story. They were either locked up or unofficially guarded by a resident misfit bachelor who lived in a shack at the premises.

The farm horses sometimes presented an opportunity when they were pastured. One in particular was kept in a field that had a lot of hawthorn bushes not only in the field but along the fence line. Hawthorns were an attraction for both the horses and the free ranging milk cows because of their tender leaves. Both animals were so attracted to them that the trees were cropped so frequently that they looked like shrubs.

One of our neighbors across the *crick* kept his horse in a pasture that had a barbed wire fence and a lot of hawthorns growing along the fence line. My oldest brother frequently walked the railroad tracks that went along this fence when he went trout fishing in the clean waters upstream.

He had a reputation for being a creative thinker, and an idea came to him when he saw that a large section of the fence was completely hidden by the low hawthorns. He quickly concluded that if the fence were cut in this area, the horse taken out, and the cut wires hooked together, the owner would not notice it because he would assume that the horse was grazing or lying down somewhere in the scrubby field. He also concluded that this could only be done on Sunday, when the owner strictly observed the Sabbath.

He tried the scheme the next Sunday, and it worked perfectly. After riding the horse where it would not be observed by the owner, he would open the wire and put it back in the pasture. He did this occasionally for a few years before he went off to the college.

Years later he had a conversation with the owner who said, "I need to ask you a question. I know that when you were younger, you would take my horse and ride it, and it would be tired when I used it on Monday morning. How did you get the horse out of the pasture without using the gate near the barn?"

When the hidden break in the fence was explained to him, he grinned and they both had a good laugh. The truth be known, he had more than a little larceny in him himself and probably admired a good horse thief—even a borrower.

Chapter 19

Outhouses

They were referred to by many names, from the crude term "shit house" to the more refined "toilet." When some of our cousins visited from the big cities, they called them "crappers," but we never adopted the term because we had no admiration for the speech of our big city relatives.

The architecture of the shit house was basic. A structure of some sort was built over a hole in the ground. Usually it was made of vertical rough sawn boards topped by a slanted roof like a shed. The door was made of the same plank material. A more upscale model had horizontal house type siding, but this was typically used only in a commercial establishment or a schoolhouse. I never saw one built of bricks, although the term "built like a brick shit house" was frequently used in reference to a well-stacked girl.

Interior size was determined by family structure, and the terms one-holer, two-holer, and three-holer, etc. were common. Holes sizes were based on family structure, with small holes for the toddlers and large ones for the grownups. The holes were sawed into a plank bench, and a fancy store-bought seat was really rare.

Usually the spaces between planks provided adequate ventilation, but those with an artistic inclination sometimes sawed out a star or crescent. However, these were not common and looked upon as pretentious.

Each outhouse acquired an identity of its own because of the aroma it developed. Also, the calling cards of those who went before you could be identified by sight and smell. When a hole became too full, a new one was dug alongside, and the house was moved by nailing some lifting planks to the sides so that four strong people could lift and move it horizontally.

Store bought paper was not used. A Sears catalog was standard equipment, and the softer index pages were always the first to go. You then worked your way through by texture, and when you had nothing but slick colored pages left, it was time to look for a new catalog.

Business establishments that used outhouses generally had a "Men" and "Women" door inside the places of business such as a bar. When you opened the door, a path led to two shit houses marked by sex. The farm people usually thought this was a needless extravagance and joked about the highfalutin' ways.

Sometimes during the rainy season, the out houses seeped a liquid that smelled. I recall an event where the seepage was visited by honeybees who gathered something from it and made a beeline for the hives a few houses away. I always looked upon honey with suspicion after that, but found out later that bees kill bacteria during honey production, so the human population was not harmed. It still was an interesting phenomenon.

Years later a friend in college told a story about a traveling salesman in Kansas selling stink proof shit houses. When a farmer customer questioned how this was possible, the salesman gave him a guarantee. On his next visit, the farmer confronted the salesman and told him the shit house stunk like every other one he had used.

Being fast on his feet, the salesman said that he would examine it and afterward, with a stern demeanor, informed the farmer that the reason it stunk was that someone had shit in it. So much for functionality.

You can still see an occasional shit house in the plateau, but mostly you see broken down and decaying remnants. This change did not go unnoticed. Like one of the older natives observed, "We used to eat inside and shit outside. Now we eat outside and shit inside." Shit happens.

Chapter 20
A Cow Named Lady

While I was growing up, we always had a dairy cow named Lady. The name was passed from each generation and applied to cows that were in the family long before I was born. During my childhood, I remembered two. One was a Holstein that was sold to a butcher after she became old.

I don't recall it, but I was told that when the cow was hauled away, my mother cried for days because she had lost a dear friend. She always insisted on doing the milking, except for brief periods when we would learn how to do it, so she became more attached to the cows. In her old country ways, a cow was a prized possession and source of daily nourishment, so the attachment was more than superficial.

In the Polish peasant culture, cows were not worshipped but held in high esteem. For example, my mother gave the cows a pink-colored wafer on Christmas morning that was part of those used in the sharing ritual the evening before. I think this custom may have been a carryover from the pre-Christianity days, when the peasants worshipped an earth mother from whom all life came.

The name Lady passed on to a Guernsey that was the one I best remembered as I was growing up. This is the one I would lead to pasture, and it always took a long time because I would let her stop to strip the leaves off the hawthorn shrubs that grew along the road. She would gently tug the rope toward the bushes, and I didn't have the heart to refuse her.

We also used a pasture that was farther up the valley in the village. Each morning we led the cows there by a short rope and then went for them in the evening. As they were walking toward home, the exercise apparently stimulated their bowels and they each shit at the same place along the highway. Unfortunately, the place was right in front of the door of a house located right on the road. The residents got so perturbed that they would come out and try to hurry the cows, but the consistency of the biological clock made it a useless exercise. We, of course, could do nothing but watch and be inwardly amused at the whole thing.

When the cow pies dried, they could be easily lifted with a shovel, so no permanent harm was done. A beekeeper even used them for insulating hives.

We had no breed bull, so whenever the need arose, someone had to lead Lady to a farmer who had one so that a mutually desirable event, or usually, events, could occur until the bull was spent and Lady was satisfied. My father or one of the older brothers usually did this task, but when we grew older, my brother and I led Lady to the bull. We noted that she always went willingly, or with great enthusiasm, and on the return trip she seemed to have undergone a complete change of personality.

As a calf grew in Lady, milk production slowed and then stopped completely until the calf was born. A new calf was always an adventure. Sometimes they were born in the barn, but frequently they were born as the cows roamed the woods or pastures. It was always amazing to see a calf start walking soon after being born, but when not born in the barn, they usually had to be carried home if the distance was far.

Calves were never named unless they were being kept to grow into dairy cows. If they were not going to be raised, after weaning, they were either sold to someone who wanted to raise them, to a butcher for veal, or were butchered at home. Sometimes they were kept to be yearlings before they were butchered, which we called baby beef.

Lady's offspring did not always resemble her in appearance or temperament, apparently because of the genes provided by a bull of questionable background. One of her calves, a jersey named Cherry, that we raised as a second milk cow, was a bit jumpy or hyperactive.

One day, while I was leaning over to give Cherry a bucket of water, she reared her head up quickly. Although I jerked back in reaction, one of her horns caught me on the bridge of the nose, and cracked my skin right near my eye socket. If the hit had been one inch higher, it would have taken out an eye. I thought it was one of those times when God, or a guardian angel, or both, was looking out for me.

After butchering a yearling or calf, the hide was sold. Usually, the word got around that a hide was available, and a dealer would show up at the house to examine it and bargain on a price. We always assumed that the dealers had an excellent markup because they showed up about a day or two after the butchering.

We had butchered a yearling one fall, and true to form, a dealer showed up early one morning a couple of days later. I was carrying water to Lady while my father was unrolling the hide for the dealer to look at. I had the bucket in front of Lady and she was drinking. She was facing in a direction where she could look out of the barn door.

When my father and the dealer unrolled the hide and each held an end to stretch it out so they could see the size, Lady saw it and jerked in reaction to recognizing it as her calf. She stared at it, and a large teardrop formed at the bottom of one of her eyes and rolled out onto her face.

Chapter 21
An Easy Place

They were known by colorful names like Bicycle Mike and Dirty Mike. They were misfits of one kind or another, but they served a purpose in life. They were coal mine bachelors, who "bached" in shacks right at the mines.

They were a source of cheap labor, and even when idle, their presence served as security for the property and mules. They expected little in life, and their expectations were greatly exceeded. Theirs was a life of minimal ambition and even less responsibility. Money for drink and food was earned, and a dry place to sleep was provided by the mine owners as part of their reward in life.

Women had no place in their lives by the time they had degenerated to this state, and numbered among them were two drunkard wife-beating brothers who had been exiled to this bituminous Elba.

None owned a car, a suit of clothes, a white shirt, nor more than one pair of shoes. They paid no taxes, did not attend church, and voted only when the mine owners provided transportation and instructions on how to mark the ballot.

Money received on payday was spent for drink after paying the grocery and clothing tab run up since last paid. Food was delivered to the shacks by merchants who charged what they wanted but for the most part were honest. In their hearts they felt human love for the free spirits and in some ways envied them for their freedom. They would not for the world have changed places but must have thought of the bachelors as they themselves plodded faithfully on the treadmill of conventional life.

Their shacks were made of rough sawn native lumber, with two rooms. One served as a kitchen and a place to sleep, and was heated with a wood and coal burning cook stove. The second room, intended as a bedroom, was used to store dry wood fuel and miscellaneous possessions. Electricity was not available, and lighting was by kerosene lamp.

The walls were board and batten and uninsulated. The roof was cheap tar paper. Two small windows were provided, and the door was made of the same rough wood as the walls.

Ventilation in summer was no problem, and cheap, namely free, coal made up for the drafts in winter as long as the bachelor woke frequently enough to stoke the stove.

Water was provided in drums from the supplies delivered for the mine mules. Much was not consumed even though coal mining was filthy work. The philosophy of "why wash today when you will only get dirty tomorrow" was popular, and one bath in a washtub before going to town on payday was enough.

A crude outhouse located near the shanty served for basic needs, and the production of one person made it unnecessary to move it to a new hole. Stepping outside of the door to urinate often substituted for even the short trip to the privy.

Cooking usually amounted to adding new items to a pot that always stayed on the stove. A good pot had an accumulation around the top that was a living history of what had been cooked for months. If the accumulation got to be too much for even the tolerant cook to stand, it was scraped off into the fire and a new history was started.

Coal mining clothes were never washed, but wore out in their natural state. It was commonly believed that washing them only made them wear out quicker. If you were not too picky, the going-to-town clothes could go at least a year between washings, and if they happened to wear out first, they were replaced.

Sleeping accommodation was normally a couch that

exhibited an accumulation of coal dust. If it got to the point where even the bachelor could not stand it, a new layer of something clean was added on top. Bugs were not a problem, and the popular belief was that the coal dust and its sulfur content served as a natural repellent.

A trip to town on payday was made with the "boss" after getting cleaned up. The first stop was at the grocery store, where the outstanding bill was paid and arrangements were made for a new "order" and a ride home the next day if the miner did not get home that night. The next stop was at one of the ethnic clubs, a commercial bar, or the American Legion, depending on the bachelor's background. Drinking, and sometimes playing the slots at the Legion followed until the miner ran out of money.

If not drunk, the long walk to the mine was made at night. If too drunk to walk, any available place to sleep it off was used. This was frequently the store owner's barn, and a ride to the shack was taken the next day with the merchant delivering the groceries.

Because no money was now available, and credit was not given for drinking, alcoholism was not a problem. You could say that these free spirits were truly social drinkers.

A typical bachelor was Dirty Mike, whose real name was Michael, with the nickname bestowed by description. He had lived at several mines, and we got to know him a little when we took long walks in the woods on Sundays. He was generally friendly, but seldom talked about himself.

Dirty Mike at the door of his Elba

One Sunday, when relatives were visiting, we drove to where he lived. He was a bit suspicious but eagerly became talkative when we gave him two bottles of beer, a windfall he did not expect until next payday.

He quickly drank one and sipped the second. He asked who we were because we had some older brothers with us. He remarked that my oldest brother must have an "easy place" because he was a bit chubby around the middle. A "place" is a miner's term for the location at the end of the tunnel where he personally is responsible for producing mined coal. An easy place is one where the coal is high, the "roof" is strong, the drainage is good, and the distance to the main tunnel is short. We all had a good laugh, and the term stuck and was used whenever anyone put on a little weight.

One of the more colorful characters was Bicycle Mike, so named because he got a Whizzer motor bike and could get to town more frequently. He managed his money with greater care, seldom got drunk, and was generally cleaner than the others.

He was also different in that he dressed in women's clothes in and around his shack. Some thought it was because of a memory of his lost wife, but as we became more knowledgeable of the world, we found out that things were a bit more complicated.

I remember being struck with terror one Sunday as I was walking up a dirt mine road to go trout fishing. As I rounded a turn, I saw Bicycle Mike walking toward me dressed as a woman. His bike was apparently broken, and he was going to town. I later assumed that he would have taken off the dress and bonnet he was wearing when he got nearer civilization.

When he saw me, he quickly ran off the road and stood behind a bush. I had the presence of mind to pretend that I did not see him, and I looked straight ahead and walked beyond where he was. The whole time, the hairs were standing up on the back of my neck, and I thought of the words about whistling past the graveyard.

At that time, I could not have whistled if I had tried. I also recall that I did not enjoy my fishing that day.

You can imagine what an ugly male dressed in a gingham dress and wearing a bonnet looked like to a teenage boy. Later in life, I marveled at how well I had reacted and how much self control I had possessed.

When the mines closed, nearly all the bachelors disappeared and probably went to the county "poor house." Only Dirty Mike remained because he had some kind of veterans pension and the mine owners let him live in a shack on the abandoned property. As years went on, he became more feeble, and on a grocery run, a store owner found him frozen to death in his shack.

Today, the shacks have decayed and fallen and nature has nearly obliterated their presence. If you know where to look, you can still see the free spirits in your imagination and wonder if they are looking down with awe on a world that bears little resemblance to that in which they lived. Maybe they have finally found an "easy place."

Chapter 22
A Few Bricks Shy of a Full Load

Around our town, the expression was usually that a person "didn't have all of his marbles." This form was common because marbles was a popular schoolyard game, played in several variations and either for "fun" or for "keeps." Only the highly skilled contenders played for keeps because the rules were strict and the innocents were quickly parted from their marbles. General scarcity of money and the economy during the depression didn't permit the purchase of new ones to replace those that were lost.

People did play cards, so it was common to hear that a person was "not playing with a full deck," and the truth be known, some of the kids really did play cards with a deck that was less than 52. The games were only for fun, so it really didn't much matter if a couple of cards were missing.

I never heard the expression that a person's "elevator didn't go all the way to the top" until I moved away, probably because we didn't have an elevator in our town and using elevators was not a common act.

We did have a brickyard in town, and there were two more about four miles away, so the expression of "being a few bricks shy of a full load" was fairly common. In the right hands, it could be skillfully woven into a story.

One of our old timers told the story of an inbred hillbilly family with six male members who worked together in one coal mine. Each morning they would walk to the mine in line with the father in the lead and the boys following him according to age. They had aluminum lunch buckets on their arms and were already bowed from the waist so they wouldn't forget and bump their heads when they entered the mine tunnel.

One morning the oldest son, who was walking right behind the father, started whining about something not being right. When Pa asked him what was wrong, he said that his younger brother, who was farther back in line, was screwing his wife and he couldn't get him to quit. Pa looked back at the younger son, then sucked in his cheeks and spit on the ground. He then looked the oldest in the eye and said, "Look at it this way, son, at least it's in the family." This group could accurately be described as being a few bricks shy of a full load.

An interesting variation on this expression occurred

during the great depression, when jobs were scarce and sometimes employers demanded special favors when hiring people.

A story widely told concerned an immigrant named Pete going to see Jiggs Flanagan, a redheaded Irish superintendent, or "boss," about a job in a mine. Jiggs didn't invite Pete into his house because his wife was home, but he talked to him outside on the porch. Jiggs was very short and had a strong resemblance to a frog. He got his nickname from the comic strip character because of the fancy way he dressed for church on Sunday.

He had to look up at his visitor when he talked. He told Pete that he would think about hiring him and that Pete should send his wife to meet Jiggs down by the swamp that evening, and he would pass his answer to her.

Pete thought about the offer on the way home. He was desperate and explained the situation to his wife when he got home. She was also desperate and reluctantly agreed to meet Jiggs at the swamp. When she got there that evening, Jiggs was waiting and quickly made his intentions known.

She was a tall husky woman, and Jiggs had to look up at her also. As he got more amorous, it dawned on him that his picking the swamp as a meeting place, especially during the spring thaw, was a bad choice, for there was not a dry place to lie down.

He stood on his tip toes and tried to do it standing

up, but the best he could do was to get within about four inches of where he needed to be. By this time, he was really hot, and necessity being the mother of invention, he asked Pete's wife to wait right there while he went looking for some bricks that he could stand on. He had remembered walking past a pile of them on his way to the swamp.

When he went to get the bricks, Pete's wife got disgusted and went home. She told her husband about what the "zaba," or frog, had tried to do, and they both had a good laugh and were relieved that she did not have to go through the whole experience. Jiggs also went home when he returned with an armload of bricks and found her gone.

The next day, Jiggs sent word to Pete that he had the job, apparently hoping that Pete would be grateful and not spread the story about what had happened. However, the story was too good, and quickly made the rounds. Afterward, when people would use the expression about being a few bricks shy of a full load, some of them would get a funny grin on their faces.

Chapter 23
The Games Men Play

Much of what amounted to recreation on the plateau was invented. In the summers during the 1930s, local baseball became popular because it did not cost much and the population was high enough to assemble teams in villages that were within walking distance of each other.

There were many small clearings where the free ranging milk cows grazed when they were let loose to roam in the morning. In these open areas, the cows cropped the hawthorn trees so that they turned into low shrubs. After a fairly level clearing was selected, it took some work with an ax, pick, and hoe to remove these bushes and create an infield. The outfield was usually poorly defined, and sort of transitioned into the woods because the willingness to work hard went downhill rapidly as soon as the infield was completed.

Home plate and the bases were made of the best flat rocks available, and it was not uncommon for outfielders to dodge rocks and shrubs when in pursuit of a ball. Some fields had backstops made of timber poles and chicken wire.

In spite of the crude facilities, the local villages competed with enthusiasm and generally got along well even though the umpiring was sometimes suspect. Nobody could recall an incident where the owner of the ball and bat quit and took them home. Not everyone had baseball gloves, and many a "hot" ball was caught barehanded.

As darkness came on, and the games were over, some people gathered wood and built small fires around which they sat to tell stories and converse. Usually, these groups were male only, and the stories had no limits for content.

Sometimes hunger would set in, and the topic would turn to how to get something to eat. When corn was in season, a few people would be sent to a nearby field to bring back some roasting ears. Another source was freshly dug potatoes when they were in season. But the most adventurous food was chicken stolen from someone's coop.

Cooking a chicken over an open fire took a bit of work. First, a bucket of water had to be boiled to scald the chicken and separate the feathers from the skin. Then the head, feet, and innards had to be removed. Few of the thieves had the patience to broil a chicken on a spit, so the bucket or an old pot was usually refilled with water, and the chicken was boiled until it became tender.

If a bottle of local moonshine got the social group a bit mellow, preparation of the chicken was not always done with care. On one occasion, a member of the group was demoted when corn started to float to the top of the water as a rooster boiled, because the craw had not been removed.

The village chickens were what are now known as range chicken. In the summer, when the gardens were newly planted, the hens and roosters were kept in an enclosure made of poles and chicken wire. After the gardens grew to the point where they could not be harmed, the flock ranged freely in the farmyard and beyond. Their freedom led to humans frequently stepping in droppings, which likely led to the expression "chicken shit" to describe something disgustingly unpleasant.

Their movements gave rise to the expressions of "Why did the chicken cross the road?" and "When the chickens come home to roost." When the chicken did not successfully cross the road, there was usually fresh soup that night for dinner. It was not always enjoyed with gusto when the manner of death was brought up.

Automobiles were not the only hazard the chickens encountered. Some would occasionally enter a pigpen searching for grain. If they were not wary, a hog would occasionally nab one and leave only the wing tips and a few feathers when it was finished chomping on it.

Killing chickens for food took several forms. The preferred method was to grasp the victim by the legs with one hand and pinch the wing tips and legs together with the same hand. The neck was then placed on a wooden chopping block, and the head was lopped off with a single cut with a hatchet or ax. The body was held until it bled out and the chicken was dead.

Some people preferred to let go of the chicken after the head was cut off. The chicken then flapped about and ran around until it bled out and died. This technique led to the expression "Running around like a chicken with its head cut off."

The crudest form was to wring the neck. The head was held, and the body was twirled until the head and body separated. The chicken then flapped about until it died. Among purists, this was thought to be a barbaric form of killing.

Chicken theft was a highly developed art form and took skill to accomplish without getting caught. Most owners were wise to the possibility and had fairly sturdy coops that they kept locked. However, the thieves were equally creative and generally knew the safeguards that each owner used.

One owner had a coop that could be described as a fortress. He kept it securely locked at night and bragged that no one could break into it without waking him. He even showed it off proudly when someone would stop by. He did not realize that a potential thief had determined just where the roosting area was inside the coop, and had counted the boards down one side of the building so that he could locate it from the outside.

For those not familiar with the art of chicken coop building, chickens do not roost on the floor. The floor is where the droppings fall, and the birds roost on an elevated area usually made of small saplings so that they can comfortably wrap their feet around them while they sleep.

Our creative thief worked this chicken behavior to his advantage. After dark, when the chickens were sound asleep, he located the roosting area from the outside on a wall that was away from the owners house and, using a keyhole saw, carefully cut a round opening slightly above the sapling platform. He needed to do this quietly so as not to disturb the owner.

When the hole was complete, he inserted a sapling that he had brought with him and slowly disturbed the chickens by moving it back and forth. The chickens made a little noise, but when the owner looked out in the moonlight, he could see the coop door was secure, so he was not alarmed.

The thief waited for the fowl to settle down, which some of them did on the sapling that he had left inserted in the hole. He then carefully withdrew the sapling, and one by one removed the chickens and placed them in his sack. His companions at the fire had chicken that night, and some were left over for his family.

Like all good stories, this one quickly got around and the owners were alert to a repeat. Unfortunately, all chicken thieves are not smart, and the day came when a repeat was attempted. This was done by Gus, a character who was a few bricks shy of a full load.

Gus was not dumb enough to try it on the first victim, but he did not choose wisely. After he cut the hole, he stirred the chickens with vigor, and they became loud enough to wake the owner, who grabbed his shotgun and ran to the coop.

Gus heard the screen door slam as the owner left the house, and he dropped everything and took off running. The owner rounded the corner of the coop, saw Gus going full speed, and cut loose with both barrels of number 8 bird shot. Gus yelled and kept on running until he disappeared into the woods.

A few days later, the owner was talking to a neighbor and remarked that he had not seen Gus walking to town as he usually did. The neighbor said, "I saw his wife yesterday, and she told me that Gus has pneumonia." The owner smiled and said, "It's pneumonia all right, shotgun pneumonia."

Chapter 24
By Any Other Name

Coal mining on the plateau was done in two basic methods. The older was deep mining and started as an industry shortly before the beginning of the 20th century. The newer form, strip-mining, was not undertaken seriously until the World War II years of the 1940s.

The methods are pretty much as their names imply. In strip mining, the overburden of trees, soil, and various rock layers is removed, or stripped away, to expose the coal, which is then loaded on trucks and hauled to consumers or processing plants.

The older method, deep mining, was done in a variety of ways, depending upon the ease of access to the coal layers. The simplest form was to run a horizontal tunnel into a hillside at an elevation where the coal seam "cropped out," or was hidden under a shallow layer of soil. A two-man crew could employ this method and produce enough coal to make a respectable living.

When the tunnel became long enough that natural ventilation was not adequate, the simple method became more complicated with the addition of ventilation shafts and powered fans. For tunnels that were sloped into the ground to reach the coal, additional equipment, such as a hoist, was needed to drag the loaded coal cars to the surface.

Miners normally worked in two-man crews in assigned "places" to produce coal. Usually, the coal was undercut by hand or machine and then blasted down with a powder charge, after which it was hand loaded onto cars that ran on a narrow gage rail line. In some mines, the coal was not undercut, but was blasted "on solid" with dynamite, and then loaded.

As the tunnels grew in length, the coal cars had to travel a considerable distance, and ponies or mules were used to pull the cars. The ponies were what the name implies, miniature horse-like animals that were small enough to comfortably work under the low roof of the tunnel.

The "mules" were not really true mules, which were too tall to work in the mines, but were donkeys, or asses. The drivers were called mule skinners, and no self-respecting miner would let himself be called a donkey skinner or an ass skinner. Hence, the name mule was used even though it was incorrectly applied.

Mule skinners consisted of those who abused the animals to get them to work and those who were kinder and gentler and accomplished the same job without abuse or profanity. In fact, some would develop genuine affection for the animals and gave them tender care. A popular poem of questionable rhyme sums it up.

> *My sweetheart's a mule in the mine,*
> *I follow her all of the time.*
> *Whenever I spit,*
> *Tobacco juice I git,*
> *All over my sweetheart's behind.*

There was a case where affection apparently got carried away. A long time skinner nicknamed Fumble was noted for the tender care that he gave his mules. He was a topic of frequent discussion because he did not marry until he was well past his prime at the age of 70, and whenever we children asked why, our parents evaded giving a direct answer.

It was only after Fumble had died that we were told he had been having a long time love affair with his mules and had known them in the biblical sense. Being creative, we quickly made the association between a vernacular expression for sexual intercourse and Fumble's behavior. Much more literally than the expression, he had truly been getting a piece of ass.

Chapter 25
An Early Interest in Automobiles

Automobiles and trucks were items of not only use but fascination for both the young and the old. We kids loved the smell of gasoline and were intrigued by the workings of the machinery. Watching something run or observing a repair was both entertaining and educational.

Not everyone had a car. The Johnny Bull welfare cases were prohibited from owning one as a requirement for their eligibility. A lot of walking was done, and trips beyond walking distance were made on the bus or by arranging a ride with someone who had a machine that could make an all-day trip, for example, to the county seat, a distance of about forty miles. This was a location all immigrants needed to go to in order to complete the process of becoming naturalized citizens.

My father frequently made the trip, not only to

provide transportation but to serve as a character witness during the naturalization process. He ran into a humorous situation when he went as a witness for what he assumed were husband and wife neighbors. After he described how upstanding they were, the judge asked him if he knew that they were not married. He was shocked and said no. Apparently the judge had his laugh for the day, and citizenship was granted.

Even a short trip required special preparation. The tires needed to be checked for pressure and inflated with a piston type hand pump if necessary. Battery and radiator water was topped off, and the windows were cleaned.

My father was one of the few immigrants who owned a car. He operated an undercutting machine in the mine and was not afraid of learning to drive. Most of the other Slav miners were afraid of machinery, except for a few mine owners who had their own trucks and cars. However, the children of the immigrants became familiar with cars and became chauffeurs for their parents.

Our family car was a 1928 Ford Model A that was purchased right before the great depression. It had a distinctive sound and smell, and by current standards was primitive. It had no heater and required frequent maintenance. Some of the way things were repaired would be similar to the descriptions in the book *The Grapes of Wrath.*

Every time that the hood was raised or a wheel was

jacked up was an educational experience. Neighbors would drop by to watch if nearby. Adjusting the timing on a Model A was a simple procedure, but it was done with care. When finished, you could watch the distributor housing turn when the spark lever was moved. Cars were simpler then, and it seems that life was also.

During the great depression, tires were available but usually beyond what the people could afford. All possible wear was gotten from a tire, and this frequently required a repair with a blowout patch. You could buy a patch, but most were made by cutting and shaping part of a tire that was beyond use. The finished product resembled a large pancake, so it was natural the World War II GIs nicknamed the mess hall pancakes blow out patches.

Inflating tires with a hand pump took a long time and a lot of effort. There was a great temptation to check the pressure frequently with a gauge, but the more experienced pumpers just worked away at it and took their time.

My pal Ivan's family had a Ford Model T pickup truck. It was a primitive and temperamental machine and took frequent adjusting of ignition coils. It was used for local errands and was not reliable enough to take on a trip of more than a few miles. However, when the elementary school had a scrap metal drive during World War II, the Model T hauled everything to a large pile in front of the building.

There were a lot of dump trucks in our region because of the coal mines, and included simple Ford A models with hand cranked dump bodies, gross looking older Whites, and Internationals. There were a lot of late 1930s Fords and Chevrolets, which were powered by automobile gasoline engines. There was a lot of double clutching as the trucks climbed the hill alongside our farm. It made a sound that stays with you.

When my older brother and I were in our early teens, we decided to get an old engine running. This was part of a whole junk car, a 1920s Durant Motors vehicle named the Star, that had been given to us by cousins who left the area to move to Pittsburgh. It had an engine that was built by Continental, a noted manufacturer of aircraft power plants.

The car had been dismantled, and the engine was stored in a corner of the barn and had not been run for over ten years. Bits and pieces of the rest of the car, including parts of another engine, were located in other places on the property.

We found that the engine was complete except for the generator, which was driven by a gear that mated with a larger camshaft gear. The generator drive was important because it also turned a distributor mounted on its aft end.

We disassembled, cleaned, and examined everything with what now seems nearly a religious awe. Both of us were amazed that the parts were so mechanically elegant.

We analyzed everything until we had an understanding of how things worked. We frequently consulted a well-worn copy of *Dykes Automotive Encyclopedia* that an older brother had brought home from an auto mechanic trade school.

The car had used a vacuum tank fuel pump that fascinated us. It is a simple device that has a float system to use engine vacuum to draw fuel from the main tank, which is then gravity fed to the carburetor. A major drawback of this design is that it doesn't pump fuel at open throttle with low vacuum.

We eventually found a generator at an abandoned mine site where a similar engine had been used to pump water. Our prize was on a platform in the middle of a pond that was too deep and dangerous to swim or wade. We had to wait for the ice to form in winter and then claimed our needed part.

After about six months of work, the engine was mounted and running to the point where it was used for driving a flat pulley belt for various equipment. We were two proud kids when it fired up for the first time after hand cranking. We took extra pains to make sure the spark was retarded, so the crank didn't kick back on us.

After this experience, nothing mechanical was ever intimidating to me.

Chapter 26
A Spirit of Adventure

I had the same curiosity about the vast world that was out there as any other kid that read adventure stories, but I had no means to explore it in real terms. However, I had a world of unknowns nearby in the forms of the woodlands and the coal mines that were scattered in the hollows and runs. This was a good substitute and helped satisfy my spirit of adventure.

Going with the older kids to hunt for the free ranging cows in the evening got us acquainted with the nearby areas. Even this tame sounding endeavor sometimes led to a memorable experience. On one trip, I was following an older kid through a swamp that had tall reeds, and we could see only a short distance. We almost stumbled into a monstrous paper bee's nest, the kind that contains aggressive wasps. Fortunately, we backed out without disturbing them and looked for the cows elsewhere.

Having gotten acquainted with the terrain, we younger kids frequently set out on our own and explored the old coal mines that we found. On Sunday, we even visited the working mines that were taking a day off. The smell of the mule barns and pasture fields was actually pleasant and blended with the rest of the aroma of the woodlands.

In the summer, we ventured far and near to pick strawberries, blueberries, and blackberries. The locals called the low bush blueberries *huckleberries,* but there really was another bush correctly named huckleberry that bore fruit later in the summer.

The best blueberry picking was in the higher elevation where forest fires frequently happened. The fires cleared out the ferns, and the newly sprouted berry plants got more light and had better fruit. Some of these berry picking trips took us farther from home than we had ever been.

Hunting also expanded our knowledge of the terrain. At first we went with someone older, but I, in particular, like to gradually expand my known territory by going a little beyond what I already knew. Deer hunting covered the most territory and took us into the higher runs where the water was clean.

You could see a fire lookout tower from our house. It was about five miles away on the highest ridge on the Allegheny Front. I had never been there but my curiosity grew as I became older. I had been within about a mile and a half of the tower during our deep woods deer hunting in a group, but I decided that I would visit it on my own. It was late in winter and the snow cover was about ten inches deep.

One Sunday, I decided to be adventurous, and set off walking from the house. I walked up the run to the farthest point that I had been deer hunting, a place where the stream made a sharp turn to the left, so it was called the big bend. There were no other human tracks in the snow, so I knew I was alone. I decided to go up the run until reaching the high ground where the tower was located.

I was confident because I knew that if I became lost, I could always retrace my tracks in the snow. With a bit of apprehension, I set off up the run and remember being intimidated by the steep hillsides on each side. Farther up the stream, I met a trail that crossed it and knew that the tower was on the higher ground to the left. When I came to the top of the hill, I could see the tower beyond a low growth of scrub oak.

I walked directly to the tower and when I got there, looked up, and saw a man sitting on the second set of stairs. He was surprised to see me there but said that he watched me approach. I didn't know him but we chatted for a while. He had walked in on the access road that led to the tower.

We both then climbed the stairs until I got a good view of where I had come from. I could just see our house and got a good sense of direction. I decided to save some time by walking straight down the top of a long ridge on the right side of the run. This would cut my distance considerably, and I wouldn't get as tired walking through the deep snow.

I set out confidently, kept a good direction and knowing that, if I erred, I would come to a hillside on either side of my intended track. After about a mile and a half, I came to terrain that was familiar. The trip home was uneventful. When my parents asked me where I had been, I said, "Just out for a walk." Little did they know that I was alone in the winter woods acting like a mountain man exploring the Rockies.

Chapter 27
Small Game Hunting

The different ethnic groups competed in nearly everything, but their love of hunting broke down cultural barriers and made them equals in the woods, where a man's worth was judged by how he hunted, the game that he took, and how he shared with his fellow hunters. Their small game hunting was usually done in groups and was dominated by pursuit of the cottontail. A chase with a beagle dog was a major event. Even more admired was a hunter's ability to spot a "settin'" rabbit and take its head off with a blast from a shotgun, or better yet, to call over a partner who had a 22 rifle to shoot it in the head and save a costly shotgun shell and ruin less meat.

The sportsmanship of shooting a sitting rabbit was seldom discussed, but sometimes the subject came up. I remember a time in my early teens when I was hunting rabbits with Doc. I was the one carrying the 22 rifle, and we were taking a breather when I mentioned that I had read recently that some people did not shoot sitting rabbits.

"What do they do?" Doc asked with a curious look.

"They scare them into runnin' and then they shoot them with a shotgun," I replied.

Doc gave me a funny look, sucked in his cheeks, and spit on the ground. "Them fellers must be a few bricks shy of a full load, and they don't know much about huntin' and eatin' rabbits, if you ask me," he said.

In a moment, he continued, "First of all, it ain't easy to spot a settin' rabbit. Second, if it runs, three things can happen. You can miss it, you can wound it and it might run in a hole, or you can shoot the meat full of BBs." He thought a bit longer, grinned, and added, "You don't s'pose they do the same thing with a standin' deer?" I grinned back at him, and we moved on through a blackberry thicket. I knew then that we were not hunting cottontails. We were huntin' rabbits usin' Appalachian rules.

Chapter 28
The Boys and the Deer

Deer hunting on the Allegheny Plateau is pursued with a passion. It is a good thing that the season is relatively short, or it could become addictive. Hunting is discussed in casual conversation throughout the year and involves planning and construction of tree stands, including scouting of good areas.

Sometimes it is pursued in a spirit of dogged determination, which to the outsider would appear to be beyond all reason. An example of the passion that can be exhibited by a couple of teenagers follows.

The sun that bleak December day, did shine down on the earth through clouds of gray. This rephrase of Whittier went through my mind as I stepped off the bottom tread of the porch stairs into twelve inches of newly fallen snow. I gazed at the sky as I picked the "bird shit" from the corners of my eyes. A light snow was still falling and looked like it would go for a while.

My older brother had no such thoughts as he stepped into the snow. He didn't read much other than what was compulsory in his school work and did not have the reputation of being as deep a thinker as I. He was charged up with the excitement of having a day off from high school to go deer hunting on what seemed to be a perfect day for it.

He carried a 30-30 Winchester Model 94 that had a local reputation for taking many deer. It originally belonged to our oldest brother, who bought it new in 1940, and then passed it on to the younger boys when he customized an 8 mm Mauser that he brought back from World War II. Both of the younger boys prized the rifle, but the older had first choice on it because that was part of the Appalachian rules that prevailed in such matters.

I carried a full military version of the German 8 mm Mauser that my brother-in-law brought back from the war. I had first fired a few rounds from it the day before, which was a Sunday, and remembered that it shot high even with the rear sight lowered as far as it would go. I wondered if the rifle had really been used to kill anyone in the war. My brother-in-law let me borrow it because he had killed a buck on the first day of the season, which was a week earlier.

The year was 1946. My brother was a senior, and I was a sophomore. We had the day off because of some teachers' conference, and both were of the opinion that the teachers should have conferences that covered the whole two weeks of buck season. However, we were thankful for the extra day and walked toward the woods with enthusiasm and growing excitement.

We walked along the railroad tracks which led to a trail that crossed Penn Five swamp and a small clearing where people caught grasshoppers in late summer when they went trout fishing, and then to another trail that led along Trout Run to the highlands.

There was no particular reason to use the tracks; it was just the way everyone did it when they headed in that direction. In summer, when going trout fishing the same way, the kids would see how long they could walk the rails before losing balance. No one claimed to have done it for the full three fourths of a mile.

We crossed a few deer tracks in the swamp but did not follow them. We were headed for what was known as the "big woods." This was where the deer were more concentrated and obviously where we believed the bucks to be.

When we got to Trout Run, we noticed some nearly snowed in tracks leaving the stream and heading uphill. We followed them and kicked out a buck that had bedded down on a bench on the hillside. In later years, we would learn that we should have been near the top of the hillside looking down, not at the bottom heading up.

We followed the tracks for a while but lost them in a jumble of more tracks. We then hunted upstream along the hillside of Gearhart, crossing a series of draws on the way to Locust Thicket, and exhibited more enthusiasm than skill. We saw deer tails frequently but were unable to get a shot at any. By noon we were really deep in the woods and tired from all the ground we had covered in the deep snow.

We crossed the stream just below the Big Bend and decided to split up and post for a while on opposite sides of a narrow point. After about a half hour, I heard the 30-30 crack a couple of times and headed over to where my brother was. He was really excited and said that he had hit a buck on the other side of a draw on another point farther upstream.

We went over to where the deer had been seen and located fresh tracks and a blood trail. We determined the direction the wounded deer was headed and decide that I would slowly trail it while he crossed the stream at Big Bend and posted on the other side where the deer was likely to be seen.

The track was easy to follow because of the blood trail and the distinctive pattern made by the wounded deer. I trailed slowly and was astonished to see the buck spring from a clump of scrub oak in front of me. I quickly fired two shots at it in the general direction it was going, but really didn't aim and was not surprised to see the deer keep going.

I stopped and replaced the spent rounds and noted that the Mauser had really kicked. I decided to slow down and look ahead while slowly followed the track. The deer headed downhill to the stream bottom, and the tracks led to a clump of hemlocks and rhododendrons at Big Bend. They were covered with snow and made a perfect place for the deer to stop.

I slowly approached the rhododendrons and took small steps when nearing the edge of the clump, all the time looking ahead of the tracks. As I reached the edge, I could see the deer standing in the middle of some hemlocks sniffing at a foreleg that was dangling in an unnatural manner.

I slowly eased the safety off and aimed at the front quarters. I thought I squeezed the shot off, but probably jerked it, and was amazed when the deer took off at full speed and headed across the stream and up the hillside near where my brother was posted.

I followed the track and shouted to my brother to look out for the deer. He shouted back that the deer was too far downstream for him to take a shot. We then met and discussed the situation.

We decided that we would track for a while to see the direction the deer was taking. After determining that it was headed downstream along the top of the hill, the next plan was for him to go downstream on the edge of the hill in Locust Thicket while I followed the deer.

After about ten minutes, I saw the deer running well ahead. I took two more hurried shots and was sure they were misses. The deer was still headed downstream along the hilltop. We rendezvoused again and noted that at least it was heading toward home. By now, the bleeding had stopped but the distinctive track pattern made it easy to trail. Also, it was still snowing a little, so it was possible to tell new tracks from old.

At this point, common sense was completely overwhelmed by enthusiasm, and we aggressively pursued the three-legged deer. We followed it for about one half of a mile for the full length of Locust Thicket, at which point it left the hill and dropped down to the stream at the Little Ravine. It then went directly down a crude trail that paralleled the stream. Then it left the bottom and headed uphill on the point just downstream of Locust Thicket.

It appeared to be on a steady course back upstream toward Locust Thicket, so I tracked while my brother went back upstream and posted on the hillside. However, before long the deer reversed course and headed back downstream. I retrieved my brother, and we plotted a new strategy.

This time he would track and I would flank the tracks and try to get in front of the deer. This plan could only be undertaken if you were young and full of stamina.

The maneuver amounted to moving off to the side of the track by about 100 yards and then rapidly moving in the same direction as the deer for about 300 yards. Then, you slowly move in toward the deer track and carefully look for the deer.

This took a while to accomplish, but I eventually saw the deer standing in an area between me and the new tracker. I apparently made a noise when releasing the safety, and the deer took off running inland away from the stream.

We rendezvoused again and started tracking. The deer entered an area of pole timber, which was quite open, and it didn't stop for at least three fourths of a mile. As we approached an area of scrub oaks near the location where Cimino's Camp had been, we assumed the deer would stop in the scrubs, so we plotted a new strategy. I would again flank while he trailed.

As soon as we started this maneuver, he saw the deer standing in the scrubs and dropped it with a single shot from the 30-30. We met over the deer and congratulated each other that we had not let the wounded deer get away and die a lingering death. However, we were a little sad for the deer that had shown such a great will to live.

We noted that one front leg was broken and the area above the front quarters had a bullet graze in the hide. This was apparently the shot from the Mauser that had missed in the hemlock thicket.

After gutting and tagging the deer, we wondered what time it was. Neither had a watch, and the clouds and snow had not let us see the sun all day. We assumed it must be quite late because it was now starting to get dark.

We were now nearly four miles from home with a dead deer. The snow was about 15 inches deep. It was impossible to drive to the area, so we had to figure out how to get ourselves and the deer home. We were dead tired from all the pursuit but could see no alternative to dragging the deer with us as we took the best route home.

We dragged for about three fourths of a mile along a trail toward Gearhart Hollow, at which time it became completely dark. With the good snow cover, it was light enough to see the trail clearly, but we saw nothing ahead of us other than a long night's work.

We decided that I would go ahead home to get our father to drive to Penn Five to cut at least a mile off the dragging distance. My older brother would continue the drag at a pace that he could hold, and we would meet on the trail when the father and I returned.

I set out down Gearhart Hollow through the unbroken snow, and it soon became apparent that I was more tired than I had thought. It became an endurance test, and I played the game of taking one more step and not concentrating on the distance to go. The Mauser seemed to become heavier with every step.

I passed a smoldering fire at Christoff's Mine where some other hunter had been earlier in the day. From this point on the trail was a bit easier because it had been broken by the other hunter. I kept on, took the main road to Penn Five instead of the swamp and railroad tracks, and eventually made it home.

I explained the situation to my father, and we put tire chains on the old Ford sedan and drove about a mile to Penn Five.

We then walked back the trail and eventually came to the fire that I had seen earlier. My brother shouted at us from the fire, and we went over to him. He had dragged the deer to that point and decided that he could go no farther. In fact, he wanted to stay by the fire for the rest of the night.

Our father and I talked him into leaving and said that we would drag the deer the rest of the way. He reluctantly followed us, and we took turns dragging until getting to the car.

The drive home was uneventful, and we tired and wiser boys entered the farmhouse. A seventeen-year-old and the fifteen-year-old had learned a lifetime of deer hunting and personal endurance lessons in one day. We had pushed ourselves and the deer beyond all reasonable limits and found that we could do it and even more. In a strange twist of fate, maybe something that we learned that day influenced our lives.

The mindset that we got into during the hunt may have been a sort of time travel back to primitive roots. Except for the use of modern weapons, we pursued the wounded animal with the same zeal and determination as that of a caveman whose survival depended upon acquiring something to eat. Having gone back that far in time, we probably got a glimpse of the magnitude of the whole evolutionary process to this day.

Chapter 29
The Resilience of Nature

Much has been written about how the use of natural resources for human consumption has devastated the environment of the Appalachian Mountains, especially the regions where coal was mined. In the short term, many of the observations are valid, but often overlooked is that many of the man-made changes to the environment are of relatively short duration compared to the geological age of the earth. Also, the regenerative forces of nature in the form of bacterial action and plant propagation are in continuous motion, and not taken into account when making instantaneous observations.

When the old growth pines and hemlocks that covered most of the area were harvested on the Allegheny Plateau during the 1800s, there was no environmental awareness to impede their use in expanding the industrial base of the United States and improving the human condition of the workers who toiled using hand tools and mules to bring the logs to the steam-powered mills, which employed additional people. The needed expansion of railroads also contributed to prosperity and the growth of population in the area.

Prior to harvesting, the ecology of the region was different from what it is now because the pine and hemlock trees develop a dense canopy of needles that lasts all year and prevents direct sunlight from getting to the forest floor. This results in a nearly barren environment under the trees that does not support animal life, except for creatures like squirrels and porcupines. Herbivores like deer and rabbits would find nothing to eat at any time of the year.

The evergreen stands were not completely populated by fir trees. There were some maples, oaks, and other deciduous species struggling to grow among the giant firs. However, the pines and hemlocks were dominant and prevented the others from expanding except in a few places where they had managed to get a head start on the firs.

After the firs were harvested, the terrain resembled an area that had been struck by a series of tornadoes. This is when the resilience of nature took over and, in some opinions, actually improved the environment.

When the sunlight was allowed to strike the forest floor, the deciduous trees started rapid growth and the various flowers, grasses, ferns, and shrubs that had been barely hanging on expanded and flourished. In a period of about 70 years, the hardwoods matured to the point that they were suitable for harvest, and a new timber industry developed.

By their nature, hardwoods forests are self-regenerating, so that even when a stand of trees is clear cut, new trees grow from the stumps, seedlings, and seeds deposited by the remaining trees. The result is a continuous process of renewal that provides a resource that is used by humans and provides employment for people. If you take a long view, you can conclude that the harvesting of the pines and hemlocks was a net positive for both the environment and humans. This is true especially of the environment, for the current conditions support a diversity of both plants and animals that is greater than what existed before the forest was disturbed.

In my lifetime, I have seen the hardwoods expand from relatively small trees that were harvested for pulpwood to oaks and maples that provide high quality wood for furniture and flooring, some of which is exported. Lesser grade wood is used for things like railroad ties and making paper.

Even the reverting farmland where I lived my early years is growing trees that can be harvested. This is difficult to imagine, but a cycle of about a hundred years will convert a cleared farm into a mature forest if nature is allowed to work without human interference. Robert Frost describes this process and the need for patience in a poem titled *Something For Hope*.

Deep mining of coal on the plateau started in the mid 1800s and was the primary method used up to the 1940s. It did some surface damage to the environment in the form of dumping waste slate and binder in piles that were unsightly and sometimes seeped acidic water that killed vegetation. However, the major environmental problem was the drainage from the mines themselves, which made the streams run red and killed the fish and the natural plant growth in the water. There was no regulation on when or where the pollution was allowed to run.

During the mid 1930s, when I was about five years old, I recall being able to see abandoned deep mines on the hillside looking west from our house. They were in states of decay, with the tipples rotting and falling down. Most of what was reusable had been salvaged by the owners or by the village occupants.

When we kids explored the area, we saw that new growths of trees, grass, flowers, ferns, moss, wintergreen, and shrubs like mountain laurel were creeping back upon the areas that had been trampled free of vegetation by the miners and "mules." The leaves that fell each year slowly covered the bare areas and added new soil as they decayed. After 70 years, it takes something resembling an archaeological exploration to even identify where the mines were located.

I recall one area where the mine coal cars apparently had their wheels lubricated, and there were blobs of old grease on the ground. Over the years that we explored and later hunted small game in the region, these blobs slowly got smaller and were taken over by vegetation. I later learned that there were bacteria that thrived on the petroleum-based chemicals used in the grease, and they were slowly at work eliminating it from the environment. After I was grown up and had become an Air Force pilot, I learned that an anti-bacterial compound was added to jet fuel to keep the organisms from eating the fuel and creating a residue that would do detrimental things to fuel systems. Based on my observations as a child, when I saw the grease disappearing, I was able to correlate the two events.

Polluted water drainage from the various coal seams differed. The upper layers, that we called "C" and "B" coal, had some water drainage, but usually it did not harm the streams. However, the lowest layer, the "A" coal, had drainage that ran red like wine. This apparently was caused by a pyritic rock layer near the "A" coal, and when oxygen from the air got near it, sulphuric acid was created. Directly across the valley from our house, we had an abandoned "A" coal mine that had drainage that had run into a swamp and killed all the vegetation, including the trees.

Little was done about the mine drainage for nearly 100 years. During the late 1930s, there were some WPA projects to build "French" drains at the outlets of the pollution, with the belief that they would prevent air, and oxygen, from flowing into the old mines and feeding the creation of acid. This worked to some extent, but the pollution continued to flow, as it does to this day.

Seventy years after my first observations of this pollution, you can see that the acid is more diluted, some type of algae grows in the water, and the swamp has recovered, although not to the same conditions that originally existed. Apparently, settling of the mine tunnels and the consequent natural reduction in the amount of oxygen available to the pyritic rock resulted in less acid production. As I like to tell my environmental extremist acquaintances, another two hundred years or so and the pollution will probably be gone, all as a consequence of nature taking care of things unaided. The usual response I get is that there should be instantaneous remedies for all man-made problems.

Strip mining came to our area in the early 1940s when the demand for coal increased during World War II and the labor supply decreased because a lot of people entered the military. It started out modestly, but grew in scope and exists to this day.

Early strip mining was done with relatively small

machines, and after the coal was taken, the sites were abandoned with no backfilling or reclamation. When the local population looked at this, they felt as though the pristine woodland had been devastated and nothing but ruin would prevail. However, in a matter of a year or two, vegetation began to sprout on the "spoil piles" and things like blackberries grew where the sunlight had been let into what had previously been a dark forest during the time the leaves were on the trees.

The biggest surprise was that wildlife thrived along the edges of the new strip mines and the old forest. This became a preferred area for small game hunting. Also, the new strip mining did not increase the flow of polluted mine drainage because it was done in the relatively shallow areas where the coal was not deep under the ground.

As time went on, machines became bigger, and more earth was moved to get to the coal. Fortunately, this development took place when mining became more environmentally regulated and reclamation standards became more stringent. One result of new regulations is that acid water from the reclaimed areas is nearly zero because large quantities of lime are placed in the ground during reclamation. The lime itself is a product that is recycled from coal burning power plants, where it was used to eliminate acid from the combustion process.

At the sites where the "A" coal layer was strip-mined

and reclaimed using lime, the red water drainage was eliminated. So with good planning and using sound methods, it is possible to undo the harm that was done initially. At some point in time, treatment of all deep mine drainage will be implemented, and stream quality will improve.

On the surface, the situation that exists now is that the reclaimed land is different from the hardwood forest that was there before the activity. It is nearly impossible to put the reclaimed land back into its original condition, so an alternative was developed. The approach used is to plant the land with different types of grasses and a mixture of evergreens and fast-growing species such as black locust and larch. Nature then cooperates and additional vegetation slowly propagates into the area in the form of maples, aspens, birches, and oaks that seed in from the boundary where the strip mine and remaining forest meet. Birds and other animals, including bears, also cooperate by seeding blackberries, cherries, and blueberries. Even a creature like a fox, which eats wild grapes, will cause vines to grow in what was previously a barren area. The wind also contributes in dispersing new seeds.

What you get in a relatively short time is habitat that supports more wildlife than was in the hardwood forest. Deer and wild turkeys in particular thrive in the mixture of meadows and trees. Usually there is enough original woodland between the mined areas to provide cover and support the nutrition of the traditional species.

After a lifetime of observation, I see that natural resources such as coal and timber can be used in responsible ways as long as people are environmentally conscious and reasonable. One thing you can count on is that, given enough time, nature is resilient enough to undo most of the harm that humans do in their expanding existence on this earth.

Chapter 30
Angels and Mean-Spirited Bitches

Looking back from the perspective of the early 21st century, elementary education on the plateau was primitive and unenlightened. The quality of each school paralleled the economic status of the settlements, and at the bottom of the heap was the one-room schoolhouse in the remote coal company villages, where all eight grades were taught by one teacher.

This was typically a male teacher with enough physical and mental toughness to cope with hardened young men who had no visibility on a life other than joining their fathers in the non-union coal mines. They went to school only because the law mandated it and usually quit when they reached the sixth grade. Sometimes they were in their mid-teens because of being held back a few grades. The teacher's ability to maintain discipline was considered by many to be more important than a capability to instill knowledge in young minds.

The girls in these circumstances usually stayed in school until they reached the age where they became good marriage material or were old enough to work in some low-paying sewing factory job or "go to New York to scrub for the Jews." The attitude they had was influenced by the parents, and those with little ambition passed it on to the children. I can't recall a single story of a teacher even trying to inspire students to achieve in these circumstances.

Our village had a "modern" consolidated eight-room two-story brick school building. It was located near the county line and was fronted by a state highway. Farther up a hill in front was a double track railroad that hauled coal outbound and freight inbound. Four of the eight rooms had windows on the front, and the students could look at the strangely named freight cars and dream of the world that was out there. When a freight passed, a silent game was played to see how many different cars there were. During recess, people had to defend their count by naming the different freight lines.

The rooms on the rear looked out on a rough play area that also served as a dump for the ashes that came from the coal-fired heating plant, a drainage ditch for the cesspool overflow, a single track local coal hauling rail line, a swamp, a double track rail line built on fill in the swamp, and beyond a polluted stream the town in the next county where we would go to high school. One windowless side faced a heavy machine shop that specialized in building and repairing mine equipment, and the other had a playground that bordered an abandoned mine and a wooded area. There was no playground equipment.

The second floor had a principal's office at one end above the stairwell and a mimeograph room at the other end. Each floor had a boys' and girls' restroom at opposite ends of the building. The basement was used for storage and in later years for a government subsidized cafeteria.

When you started into the first grade, your life for the next eight years consisted of moving from one room to the next until you finished all eight grades. Through the first six grades, one teacher taught all subjects. For grades seven and eight, some teachers specialized in subjects like science or music, and the students moved to the appropriate rooms.

There was a fifteen-minute recess midway through the morning and afternoon, and all students were expected to go outside, even in the middle of winter. Lunch was one hour, and those within walking distance would go home. In my early years, we brought a bag lunch that we ate at our desks and then went outdoors. When the cafeteria opened, we ate in the basement and then went out to the schoolyard. A rope pull bell, operated by the janitor, regulated the start and stop times.

My early recollection of school includes having an older sister take me to the doctor for a mandatory smallpox vaccination. This was my first visit to a doctor and I remember the strange smells of his office and the kind way he treated me. The same sister took me to registration during the summer and then dropped me off in the first grade on opening day.

The things I remember dimly are sitting quietly in my desk before class started, listening to a bible reading, standing to say the Pledge of Allegiance and the Lord's prayer—protestant version—and speaking only when asked a question or getting permission by raising your hand. Everyone had to stay seated quietly with hands folded on the desk before dismissal for recess, lunch, and the end of the day.

There was a blackboard and a portrait of George Washington at the front of each room. The upper portion of the side walls had numbers and capitals and lower-case letters strung along them. Desks were the combination seat and working area type, with an inkwell and space for books and papers.

Discipline was ironclad, and when peer pressure was added, some interesting but sad situations developed. It was possible to get permission to go to the restroom during a subject period, but few dared because of the ridicule they invited from the other pupils. In the first grade, I recall squirming and finally shitting my pants because I was too embarrassed to ask for permission. An older sibling had to be called to walk me home. I learned to plan ahead to avoid such situations again, and I went through eight grades without ever asking to go to the restroom.

One-upmanship was prevalent even among the five-year-olds. I recall having some boy make fun of my home-baked bread sandwiches when he had store bought sliced bread. I was so hurt that for a few days I tried to cover my sandwiches with my little hands so that nobody could see the bread. Looking back, I was lucky that my mother baked such delicious bread, but this didn't stop the cruelty from hurting at the time.

Because of the discipline and restraint during class periods, all the pent up energy was converted into physical activity during recess and part of the lunch hour. The smaller children played tag and invented other no equipment games. The older ones played pickup softball and football if someone brought a ball because none was provide by the school. There was real meaning to the expression about getting mad enough to "take your ball and go home." The only school sponsored game I recall is dodge ball, and one ball was shared by all eight grades.

In the winter with new snow on the ground, we played pie tag by making a pie-shaped circle and spokes, and if you started into a section of the circle, you had to continue to the next intersection, where you could wait until the "it" person in the middle made a move toward you.

Football consisted of a "pass and tag" touch game and something called kicking goals, where the opposing side had to catch the kicked ball before being allowed to kick back. I recall being backed up into the machine shop junkyard next door to the school, catching a kicked ball, and then tripping and puncturing my shin on some sharp metal. A classmate helped wash the wound with cold water, and my dad came to school to pick me up. He dressed the puncture at home and I recovered well enough to be in school the next day.

Teaching and learning were by rote. I remember the magic of learning numbers by copying them into a 10 by 10 grid that started with zero and ended with 9 in the first column, ten started the next column, etc. To this day, when I visualize numbers, I see them in a 10 by 10 form, even when they include values like billions.

After mastering the numbers, we learned simple addition and then subtraction. Multiplication tables were memorized in the second grade, and simple division was learned. As you progressed through the grades, addition, subtraction, multiplication, and long division were practiced with larger and larger numbers along with fractions and decimals. I recall being introduced to manual square roots in the eighth grade. For the most part, our arithmetic was memorized and not applied. So-called "word problems" that required moving a real problem to an arithmetical manipulation were avoided by the teachers. In later years, I came to believe that this was because they themselves did not understand them.

We did a lot of arithmetic but there was practically no understanding of mathematics learned by this method. It was only after I took algebra and geometry in high school that some concept of number theory began to soak in, and this was not taught but was personally deduced.

Subjects like history and English involved less manipulation, but memorization was still the primary form. I remember moments of enlightenment in these subjects dulled by the boredom of trying to work every arithmetic problem in the book, even when the concept was mastered and understood. We usually didn't finish the whole arithmetic book for each grade because we were so delayed by working all the problems. I sometimes wondered if the motivation was to keep us busy instead of really teaching the subject material.

Penmanship was learned and practiced using an inkwell and a nib pen. We did exercises like ovals and push-pulls, and wrote letters in both capital and lower case. We used what was called the Peterson method through the sixth grade, at which time we submitted a sample to Peterson for grading. I recall that I had the distinction of being the only student in the class who did not get a writing certificate. I did not write well and was relieved to go to block lettering in college when I studied engineering.

I recall only one science class, probably in the seventh grade. It was taught by a person with minimal understanding, and I recall an instance where we were discussing air. The teacher said that if you put five pounds of air into an inflatable ball, it would weigh five pounds more. In my own shy manner, I volunteered that in this case we were talking about air pressure, and the ball would not weigh significantly more.

The teacher asked me and another boy to conduct an experiment at home, and weigh an inflated ball. The other boy and I were considered to be competing for the smartest kid in the class honors, so we agreed.

I performed the experiment and the next day we were asked about the results. I said that you could see the needle of the scale go slightly higher, but nothing like the five pounds described. The other boy said that his ball weighed five pounds more. He rode the same school bus as the teacher, and apparently had reached an understanding that he would lie in order not to embarrass her. This was one of my early lessons in a shameless political accommodation taking precedence over facts. To this day, the other boy cannot look me in the eye.

This example was the first of many that I experienced

during my lifetime. Some people did not understand that you could not define science to meet your preconceived notions. It was just there to be understood and applied, and if you got it wrong, it sometimes came back to haunt you.

Later in life, a college professor told the story of a state legislature that believed that students' lives were made difficult because they had to use Pi in a numerical form like 3.1416, so they passed a law that it would be rounded off to 3 and taught that way. I could believe my small-town school board also doing such a thing if given the chance, but it would sure make some strange looking circles.

At the beginning of the 21st century, it seems like global warming falls into the same category, with the only rationale for believing it is that some computer models predict higher average temperatures, without understanding why they do so. Politicians are particularly adept at creating what I call pseudo science, where facts fall by the wayside of boundless ambition.

I became an avid reader as soon as I learned how and was fascinated by a view of the world beyond the one in which I lived. Each grade had a small library of possibly twenty books, and I read everything in the second grade room within a few weeks of classes starting. I then had my brothers and sisters borrow books from their grades, and by the fifth grade I had read everything in the school. I then had my high school siblings bring books home, and I read everything in the high school library before I got there.

You need to understand that both the elementary and high school libraries had a grand total of possibly 400 books, so this was no great feat. In later years, I wondered why the school boards did not support more investment in libraries. It was probably because the members themselves were not serious readers and had the limited vision of people in small villages and towns. Some of them probably did not even finish high school, but this did not disqualify them from being elected to the board.

Who were the teachers who ran this institution of learning? At the time I was there, they fell into a broad category that consisted of angels at one end and mean-spirited bitches at the other. There were various degrees of each in between.

Looking back from the perspective of seventy years, they were a cross section of humanity that was a product of heredity, upbringing, and physical and emotional baggage typical of small-town and rural America. When raising my own children, I frequently ran into the liberal view that all teachers were capable, dedicated, and scrupulously fair and unbiased. I imagine the same belief was held about my own mentors, and I knew it was an idealistic view far from the truth.

Teachers were hired by the school board, and the principal had some say in who got the jobs. The final selection was made by the board, and their choices reflected their own values and concepts of suitability. As mentioned earlier, the board members were elected, and some had little knowledge of subject matter. From my point of view, mediocrity would beget mediocrity, and we did not excel as an educational institution.

Although I was usually bored to tears, I mastered the reading, writing, and arithmetic fundamentals and assumed that most of the others did. Little did I realize that many of my classmates were barely getting any of the subject matter, and as long as they were not causing trouble, nobody seemed to care what they were learning. In later years, I had some friends comment about "Where were the teachers when I needed them?"

The ethnic conflicts of the region carried over into the classrooms, and some teachers showed their prejudices sometimes openly and frequently in subtle ways. Picking favorites for demonstrations and errands always resulted in someone other than a Slav kid being chosen. For distribution of instruments used in what was called a rhythm band, the Slav kids always wound up with a simple rattle.

This carried over even into high school, where valedictory addresses at graduation were the norm until Slav kids started taking the top honor. The policy was then changed so that the class president gave the graduation speech, with the understanding that no Slav kid would dare run for president.

This was carried so far that the printed graduation programs quit showing valedictorians and salutatorians, as did the press releases. For my graduation, an ethnic Russian girl was valedictorian, and I was salutatorian, but the press release didn't mention it, and we were all lumped into the category of honor students.

Even this slighting of achievement was not enough. At the baccalaureate ceremony held at the Methodist church, the minister gave a sermon about responsibilities the new grads would have in the world. He made a passionate plea that they should not worship learning, as if it were an idol that took the place of a real God. Even at my tender age I knew that he was telling the Methodists what they wanted to hear, and that they should be proud that none of their souls was in jeopardy by having achieved some degree of excellence at academic subjects. I actually felt sorry for such a narrow-minded individual.

The Presbyterian minister's son, who was a good friend of mine, was also an honor student, so I guess he too fit into the category of a heathen idol worshipper. Maybe there was a pecking order among the Protestants that I didn't recognize at the time. On second thought and after all these years, it dawns on me that he may have been included because he took the ethnic Russian valedictorian to the prom instead of the Methodist girl he had been dating.

His father came to the Presbyterian church a year before graduation, and the town in eastern Pennsylvania where he had been a minister had no Catholics or significant minorities. He may have really broken an unwritten rule the Protestants had. Also, he may have not been in town long enough to recognize what was going on.

As we were walking out of the church, one of the other graduates asked me how I liked the sermon. I didn't say anything, because I was already instilled with the belief that it was bad manners to point out boorish behavior in others.

A brief history of the ethnic mix of the region may provide a deeper understanding. The original settlers of the area were of English extraction with some German mixed in. The area was slowly populated after the American Revolution when veterans were given land warrants in exchange for military service. As the primary export of the region became timber, this mix continued until late in the 19th century, when soft coal took over from the depleted timber as the primary commodity.

Labor strife between the descendants of the original settlers and the mine owners led to the importation of eastern European labor of Polish, Czech, Slovak, Russian, Ukrainian, and Lithuanian extraction. These Slavs worked for lower wages than the originals, and the animosity generated lasted well into the 20th century and can still be found to some slight degree.

The expansion of the coal industry led to increased use of railroads, which attracted Irish immigrant labor, some of whom ended up owning and working in coal mines. Some of the Slavs ended up owning mines, but none competed seriously with the larger mines run by the original robber barons, who exploited labor until the union movement became stronger during the 20th century.

The perceived pecking order was the original Johnny Bulls looking down on the Irish and Slavs, the Irish looking down on the Slavs, and the Slavs looking down on some of those within their own divisions. However, the Slavs tended to be somewhat united because they together initially composed a minority but slowly out reproduced the others.

There were, of course, some additional minorities in the nearby town, consisting of a few Italians, Jewish business owners, and people of French extraction. Also, the brickyards imported their own Negro labor, and the whole thing was a strange mixture indeed. We had no Jews, Italians, or blacks in my elementary school.

The ethnic animosities carried over into the classrooms, but some teachers had kind hearts and did not stereotype the tiny tots. The first grade teacher was an old maid, as were seven out of the nine, if you counted the principal. However, she taught reading, writing, and arithmetic well and did not show any ethnic animosity. She had a technique of licking a gold star and pasting it on your forehead if you did something well.

The old maids were expected to lead lives that were above criticism, but as we grew older, we concluded that they suffered from a lack of meaningful male companionship. The first grade teacher in later years apparently reached the same conclusion and had a married boyfriend visit on weekends. However, she was discrete enough and respected for her teaching ability, so everyone politely pretended that they did not notice.

The second grade teacher was kind hearted and treated all but the troublemakers with respect. I recall an occasion when I came to school with a running cold, and she gave me her perfumed lace handkerchief because I had none. She married in her late thirties, and even we tiny tots thought that her husband was getting a good catch.

In the third grade, we had a chubby old maid, but she simply taught and did not cause trouble, so there is little to remember about her except that she broke a student desk by casually sitting on it. She was embarrassed because everyone thought it broke because of her weight.

A teacher on her first assignment out of college made fourth grade interesting. She had no concept of maintaining discipline except by yelling at the top of her voice. This, of course, was completely ineffective for kids that by now had figured out how much they could get away with without being sent to the principal's office for a paddling. Yes, corporal punishment was approved and available and seemed to be used more on the older kids who were not intimidated by the stern demeanor of the teachers. Many of the teachers had what we called a schoolteacher face, which resulted in a countenance that looked as though an iron nail could be bitten without cracking a tooth.

I recall getting paddled in the seventh grade for something that I did not do. During a recess, some of the kids I was standing with got bored and started throwing rocks at the windows of the machine shop next door. I swung my arm once, pretending to throw, but didn't have a rock in my hand. The principal was watching everything through a window and called all of us to her office when recess was over.

I explained that I had not thrown anything, but she said that she had seen me do it, so I got paddled on the butt and the backs of my legs like everyone else. She used an instrument made from a board similar to a piece of hardwood flooring, about three feet long with a handle carved into it prevent slipping from the hand. Of course we all remained silent, even though the strokes got harder. In later years, when reading about Churchill and his getting caned in school, I could relate to it from firsthand knowledge.

Churchill also commented about being able to empathize with convicts because he had spent years in elite boarding schools known as public schools. I understood him completely and felt much the same way.

The fourth grade teacher was handicapped from polio, and her marriage prospects were nil. I think she may have had an occasional fantasy about some of the students and possibly had a crush on me. People would say that I was a good looking kid, and once when she was explaining the use of the word rendezvous, she said that sometimes it was used for a romantic meeting, such as "I would like to have a rendezvous with you," and she looked right at me when she said it. She lasted only one year as an elementary teacher, and we were pleased for her when she got a job at a university.

The fifth grade is where I first felt open ethnic hostility. The teacher was Irish, married to an undertaker, and openly conveyed that her concept of the world was the only correct one, and all others were somehow inferior or wrong. Her demeanor became more stern when addressing the Slav kids, and I don't recall her ever saying a kind word to me. Looking back, I think this was when I became aware that idealism really does start to die out at an early age.

In this case, it didn't die but was severely wounded.

As I look back, this is where survival of the fittest started to assert itself. I knew that I was going to college, and that vision sustained me through a lot of adversity.

My oldest brother had paved the way for the rest of us by being the first in our family to get a college education. He suffered abuse in the community but had the fortitude to stick it out and show that it could be done. The success of the whole idea rested on his shoulders, and the load he carried was heavy. The courage and character that he exhibited are something to be admired.

My Slav friends were not as fortunate and were inclined to accept what life had in store for them. However, on a comparative basis, they suffered less open bias because they were not viewed as someone trying to get out of the place in life that others had selected for them.

In our adult years, I would occasionally meet one of these kids, and some would comment about me having it made. I didn't argue with them, but I thought that they had no idea of the price I paid to achieve some bit of success in life.

I was in the fifth grade during World War II, and one day the teacher proudly bragged that her brother had been promoted to First Lieutenant, and that this was the highest rank of anyone in our school zone or the nearby town. I had a brother who was a Captain in the airborne, but I didn't dare mention him to correct her, because I would have been ridiculed or called a liar. Needless to say, this was not a pleasant learning environment.

When I started into high school, I was walking home one day past the elementary school, and my Russian pal and I stopped in to go to the restroom. This same teacher rushed down the hall and demanded that we get out of the building. When she saw my Russian friend, she pointed at him and said something like, "What are you doing here, nobody in your family ever goes to high school?"

My friend had a mean streak of his own and replied, "Shut up, you stupid bitch." However, you could tell that he was hurt to the core. We didn't stop at the school after that. So much for dedicated teachers encouraging minorities to do better.

Sixth grade was my high point for ethnic animosity. The teacher was of French extraction, and her family lived a few houses up the road from my home. She apparently had been raised to believe that all Slavs were hunkies who deserved nothing in life. It irked her family that my father was the first of the immigrants to scrimp and save to send his kids to college and nursing or trade schools. By the time she became my teacher, her hatred had been honed to a fine edge.

She was not openly hostile all the time, but if an occasion presented itself, she leaped on it like a hyena. For example, we sometimes were expected to bring in a bar of soap for an art project. My mother, being frugal and in menopause, one day refused to give me a bar. When the teacher found out, she had me stand up and openly belittled me and my family with words like, "Your family thinks it is so great by sending kids off to college, and you can't even afford a bar of soap."

It took me a long time to get over this episode. You might ask why I didn't tell my parents about it. First of all, they barely spoke English, had no formal schooling of their own, and expected us to solve our own problems, even at a tender age. In later years, when they would talk about it, I found that my siblings had experienced similar treatment from this teacher. The whole time, our parents had no idea of what we were going through.

This was one of those character-building events that is as vivid today as it was then. Nothing that ever happened to me in life, in later schooling, the military, or business could equal what I experienced that day at the age of eleven.

You might wonder if I had a life-long hatred of this teacher. I didn't hate her then or later, but I didn't forgive her. I felt sorry for any human being that could be so driven by hatred that she would do this kind of thing to an innocent child. May God have mercy on her soul.

There is an expression about "Pissing on someone's grave" to bring closure to an event. Many years later, and a few years after this teacher died, I visited her grave. While I didn't physically piss on it, I did so mentally, and it helped put the whole thing in perspective. This was fifty years after I was in the sixth grade, and I felt no hatred, just pity.

During the war years, this teacher got a small taste of what was to come from the offspring of immigrants when they became empowered. She was accustomed to riding the school bus with us, and a front seat was reserved for her. Based on advice he got from his soldier brothers, my ethnic Russian pal one morning sat in her seat. She ordered him to move, and he refused. Subsequently, he was disciplined by the principal.

His older brother took the event to the school board, and it was determined that the bus was provided for the students, and the teachers had no right to ride. From that day on, our paragon of impartiality had to walk to school until she bought a car. We all quietly took some comfort from this outcome, and there was hope that justice could prevail. When we saw her walking by the house in the middle of winter, freezing her butt, we inwardly grinned.

The seventh-grade home room teacher was the science wizard with the heavy air pressure. She replaced a male teacher who had been hired when his remote coal village school closed. His approach to discipline was a bit bizarre, and he once challenged an older held-back kid to put on the boxing gloves during lunch hour. Of course, he beat the kid, but this was too much even for the backwoods school board, so they did not continue him after the end of the school year.

Some insight into teacher motivation was learned in the seventh grade. Once, we were scheduled to take an achievement exam to test us on our knowledge of Pennsylvania. The day before the exam, my younger sister and the sister of my smartest kid in the class competitor were asked to help mimeograph the exam. The teacher told them that if any extra copies were there after sorting, they could use them for scratch paper.

After school that day, my sister showed me the exam, and when I saw what it was and after glancing at a few pages, I burned it in the kitchen stove. The next day, my competitor asked the teacher about a question on the exam before we started the test. She answered it, so I assumed that they had again made a deal.

I deliberately did a sloppy job on the exam, and when the other kids asked the teacher how I had done in comparison to my competitor, she said that I had done careless work while he had done well. She looked at me in a strange way when she said it.

This was another one of life's lessons. The teachers wanted the school to look good, and journeyed into the realm of dishonesty to achieve their goal, apparently with the concurrence of the principal. From my point of view, I felt that I had done the right thing and had taught them a lesson that I could not be bought. Throughout my school years, I did not study for grades but for understanding of the material and the use to which it could be put. How I did on this exam was of no value to me.

Another lesson was that people with credentials in positions of responsibility and authority were not necessarily good at what was expected of them. I was to encounter this frequently in my lifetime and was always skeptical of people who defended their views by enumerating their degrees or years of experience.

Concerning science lessons in the seventh grade, I learned quite a bit by ignoring what the teacher said and figured things out on my own. When we had time during recess and lunch hour, we immigrant farm boys and selected others would discuss science and usually get things right. Friendships did cross ethnic lines, with the basic qualification being that you could not feel superior to someone else. My competitor for smartest kid did not join us because he was not qualified and would have been derided because of his flawed views.

The seventh grade teacher may have been scientifically slow and insecure in her job, but she had a kind heart. I remember one occasion when the class went on a spring picnic, and we walked past a store where we were expected to buy a soft drink. My consistently frugal mother would not give me a nickel for the drink, but the teacher bought one for me. This act of kindness, among others, kept her well out of the category of mean-spirited bitches.

The eighth grade teacher epitomized everything about meanness and ethnic animosity. She was descended from the original settlers and had a perpetual frown, or schoolteacher look, on her basically unattractive face. We frequently joked that she was not the kind you wanted to meet in a dark alley at night.

She was also a slapper and never passed up an opportunity to use her open hand on a student's head or face. We had a former classmate who was one grade behind us because he took a year to recover from a severe head injury when he accidentally shot off part of his skull when playing with a loaded revolver. He had a steel plate in his head and was mentally slow. Our slapper once saw him standing in the hall, and when he did not respond to her order to go to this classroom, she slapped him on the side of the head. When someone pointed out what she had done, she was momentarily mortified, but recovered and fell into her usual pattern.

One day we were working at the blackboard, and were given a problem to figure out how many days there were between two dates. Out loud, I recited the mnemonic about 30 days has September, April, June, and November, etc. She rushed over to me and slapped me hard across the face. My reaction was disbelief that such a violent act resulted from such an innocent event, and it reinforced my disrespect for her. At the time I thought, and still believe it to this day—that ethnic hatred played a big part in her response.

You might think that she and the sixth-grade teacher were the winners in the mean-spirited bitch contest, but they were surpassed by the principal. Here was a woman who had apparently dedicated her life to governing by fear and intimidation.

If you wanted to invent the stereotype of the old maid schoolteacher, she could have served as the model. A perpetual frown on an overly made-up wrinkled face, gray hair, a loud domineering voice, quickness to punish, and an air of superiority brought on by a belief that the Irish were superior to any other ethnic group in the world. I knew she was Catholic, and the contrast between her behavior and the teachings of Christ was something to behold.

In later years, I once saw a bumper sticker that said, "Thank God I'm Irish," and she was the first person I thought of. What a sad example of humanity, who passed up an opportunity to do so much good in the world, and dedicated her life to meanness and malice.

She clearly was the winner in the mean-spirited bitch contest, and if it were not for the possibility that she eventually took advantage of God's unlimited powers to forgive, she could well have earned a reserved seat in hell.

Looking back from the 21st century, I learned a lot more than the coursework in this institution of learning. Foremost was that civilization is an extremely thin and frequently fragile veneer on the primitive instincts of mankind. At one extreme, you have people who are candidates for sainthood. At the other are creatures who would instantaneously fit into the predatory jungle environment of survival of the fittest.

I learned techniques for living in the world that spanned the gap between both extremes, and they served me well. Also, it is apparent that the human spirit is extremely adaptable, and that adversities and obstacles, which at the time appear to be insurmountable, can be overcome with faith, hope, and persistence.

The school is now closed, having been consolidated into a more modern complex using up-to-date teaching methods. The building stands empty and partially converted into a failed business, with a broken white porcelain toilet outside near the front door. The sound waves of wooden paddles striking young butts, millions of footsteps and words of happiness, sadness, bitterness, and vicious bigotry have long ago been absorbed by the structure, converted into minuscule quantities of heat, and during the stillness of nights, radiated into space, from where the life giving energy first came from the sun.

All of the angels and mean-spirited bitches have gone to their just rewards, as have many of the students who trod those halls and the playground. If you walk around the place, you can get an eerie feeling, and memories flood your mind. Maybe the parts of us that we each lost there remain unclaimed.

Chapter 31
The Age of Enlightenment

As the decade of the 1930s neared an end, life on the plateau had settled into a routine that accepted the depression as a way of life. Ethnic differences prevailed, but did not generate any conflicts beyond those to which people had become inured. The Slavs were in their place except for my family, who were troublemakers because the children went off to college, a privilege exercised only by the offspring of the town doctor, dentist, druggist, and wealthy business owners.

We paid a price for being different, with the prevailing attitude being that we believed we were better than the others. This led to an invisible wall between us and the rest of the Slavs, and frequently open hostility with the Johnny Bulls and the Irish. The doctor, dentist, druggist, and wealthy business owners did not look down on us, and may in fact have grudgingly admired us for our efforts.

With the onset of World War II in Europe, things began to change. The coal mines opened up again and slowly people went back to work. This revived the railroads, and the town merchants started to prosper. A sense of relief and hope started to take hold in the area. As yet, the population did not know that they would pay a price for these good times.

The price came in the form of military service for the young men. As war for the United States became more of a possibility, enlistments in the navy and army and the draft took more of the young men from the town. An older brother, who did not live in the town, but worked as an electrical engineer about a hundred miles away, was called to active duty because he was a reserve First Lieutenant who had ROTC training in college. After Pearl Harbor, all hell broke loose and the world of the small town changed forever.

I became ten years old about a month after Pearl Harbor Day, so my perspective was that of a child, and much of what I write here is based on looking back at those years.

We had things like air raid drills and scrap metal drives. In fact, the nearby town donated its iron cannons from the park. In our classrooms, we changed the way we said the Pledge of Allegiance from the old way, where the arm was raised and pointed toward the flag, to placing the hand over the heart while facing the flag. Someone had decided that the old form was too much like the Nazi salute, and they were correct. We were instilled with the belief that anything German or Japanese was evil, and I recall hiding some made-in-Japan knickknacks in the sofa cushions at home because I felt they were unpatriotic.

There was an illiterate miner in our neighborhood who had three sons in the infantry. He would bring their letters to us for reading, and we would write his replies. I became familiar with what was called V-mail, which was a lightweight paper and envelope to cut down the weight of the letters, which later in the war were flown overseas.

The feelings of being at war were real at that time, especially when older kids we knew started getting killed and their parents began receiving the dreaded telegrams. This was a time when people hung a small flag in their front window with a star for each son in the military. The star became one of gold for a lost son.

Our small town and the surrounding villages had about thirty-five sons killed in the war, all of whom were buried in overseas cemeteries except for one who was killed in a ship fire near New York. They came from all walks of life, and no ethnic group was spared. The concept of being better than someone else did not carry over into battle, and people bled and died equally regardless of their backgrounds.

My family was fortunate in that of my two brothers in the army, one lasted through the entire war in the airborne, where he fought all the way from North Africa, Sicily, Italy, Normandy, Holland, and Germany through liberation of the death camps. He ended the war as a Major and left the army to resume his life as an engineer.

The second brother had gone to a mechanics trade school after high school and spent the war in India as an aircraft mechanic, where he was not directly exposed to combat. However, both brothers were drastically changed by their experiences, as were the rest of the town's young men who survived the war.

For most of them, their war experiences were the first time that they had been more than 40 miles from home, and they found the world to be greatly different from what their narrow view thought it to be. The perceived small town pecking order and feelings of superiority did not stand up to the grinding gears of the enforced melting pot called the United States military, where our boys met people from all over the country. For those at the bottom of the order, they quickly learned that they did not need to stay there.

Human nature being what it is, people will find a way to manipulate the system and other people to get ahead, but the draftees started out pretty much equal and were judged on their merits. Being in a strange environment and away from old friends, subjected to harsh discipline, being taught respect for superior ranks, a grueling physical regimen, learning to kill, and peer pressure essentially made new soldiers and different people of the raw recruits. For the first time in their lives, many found that they could do things far beyond their prior perceptions.

The military subjected the draftees to a variety of tests and some went to Air Corps training as pilots or navigators. One young man from our town became a Lieutenant and a navigator and was killed in the air war over Germany. The Irish schoolteacher's brother went to Officer Candidate School and became a military policeman. Some went to tank training, including the town grocery store owner's son, and he was killed in a tank somewhere in France. Most of the rest became infantrymen and found a life of violence that they would never have dreamed of.

Survival in the war had nothing to do with perceptions of ethnic superiority. Leadership ability, teamwork, simple luck, skill, and cunning counted for more than background. Bullets did not differentiate between the Johnny Bulls, the Irish, and the Slavs. The names on the town memorial in the park contain some from every group. They became equal in death, and this was not lost on the survivors.

Some of the draftees fought in the Pacific and didn't get exposed to other cultures unless they were lucky enough to spend time in Australia. Nearly all went to

Europe, where they found people they could relate to, and a few brought back war brides. Significantly, they were all viewed as American soldiers, and ethnic differences were blurred.

Their exposure to combat, wounds, death, the sufferings of other people, and the euphoria of being liberators changed them forever. There was a lot of accuracy in the World War I song about, "How you gonna keep 'em down on the farm, once they've seen Paree." In World War II, they saw a lot more than Paris, and things were never again the same.

The returning veterans, some of whom bore battle wounds, descended on the area with the confidence that victors deserved. They carried themselves with military bearing and were not of a mind to take mistreatment from those whom they had defended. They spoke, and frequently cussed, as equals, and the camaraderie of shared experiences broke down ethnic barriers as never before. Those who had remained behind still had their inborn prejudices, but they were muted by the confidence of the vets. To put it plainly, a vet was not about to take any shit from someone who had not had the same experiences.

For the first time, the Slavs asserted their right to participate in local government. One had the audacity to run for town mayor and nearly defeated a 20-year incumbent on his first try. On a more personal level, marriages across ethnic lines increased.

The change in attitude carried over to us of the younger generation. We admired the vets and emulated many of their ways. This created new confidence and assertiveness that gave us a better start in life after we left high school. This change did not happen overnight, but at least the seed was planted that grew into a new era of accomplishment for the offspring of immigrants.

The veterans with a new outlook received a windfall that significantly changed their lives. It came in the form of the GI bill for additional schooling. Those that qualified went to college, and those with lesser aptitude or ambition went to trade schools. I heard on many occasions that the example set by my father, in sending his kids to college, motivated a lot of the Slavs to do the same under the GI bill.

Not all of the vets were changed in a positive way by the war. People with instincts to scheme, steal, and get a free ride in life came back the same way. I recall my disappointment when one of the vets got arrested for stealing gasoline from parked cars. However, the positive changes far outweighed the negative, and there were more success stories than failures.

The war experiences and schooling launched this generation on a new path to accomplishment and prosperity. Some unmotivated people still worked in the mines or rail industry, but many became teachers, foresters, lawyers, accountants, and engineers. Looking back, the war years and GI bill unleashed a cultural change that it is safe to say would not have occurred otherwise. It really was an age of enlightenment.

How could a tragic event like World War II have had such a positive result? It is yet another example of the validity of the proverb "It is an ill wind that blows nobody any good." When I first heard the proverb in high school, I had no understanding of what it meant. Looking back, it applies well to the age of enlightenment.

Chapter 32
A World War II Experience

All of the boys and men who went off to war had a story of their own when they returned. Those who did not return lived on in the memories of the ones left behind and in the shared experiences of their buddies. Those who got killed are frozen in time when it comes to memories and shall forever be young. However, their sacrifices are often forgotten but occasionally preserved in writing. The following poem, appropriately titled *Sacrifice* and written by my brother-in-law, Frank, who was a combat wounded veteran, sums up the depth of their sacrifice. The book *No Greater Sacrifice, No Greater Love: A Son's Journey to Normandy* written by Walter Ford Carter, largely features Frank. Walter Carter is the son of Dr. Norval Carter who made the ultimate sacrifice when he was killed by a sniper while saving Frank's life.

Sacrifice

Young men, long gone before their time.
No more to know the warmth of a woman's love,
  or to hear the laughter of a child.
No more to see the beauty of the land, or that
  of the skies above.
No more to dream of days to be, or to enjoy the
  pleasures that life can bring.
Young men, so great your sacrifice.

My most vivid memories of World War II are based on the experiences of my oldest brother, Tony, who got called to active duty in 1940 as a reserve lieutenant when I was eight years old. He went through extensive engineer training and became part of the 307th Airborne Engineer Battalion, a unit of the 82nd Airborne Division, which operated as both parachute and glider companies. Most of his combat time was as the battalion executive officer, the headquarters of which used gliders.

The 82nd Airborne is not as well known as the 101st, which got a lot of publicity because of the defense of Bastogne, and the book and television series *Band of Brothers*. However, it had more combat experience than the 101st, having taken part in combat in North Africa, the invasion of Sicily and the campaign in Italy. Both divisions took part in the Normandy invasion, the Market-Garden battle in Holland, the Battle of the Bulge, and the campaign across Germany to the time of surrender.

The military chronology of the divisions is well documented, but the human part of what it was like varies depending upon the perspective. My memories are based on stories told by my brother after the war was over. In addition, he wrote some material submitted to Cornelius Ryan for use in his books. Copies of this material were among his estate papers. Also, his experiences are recorded in Army historical records which were used in a book *The 307th Airborne Engineer Battalion in World War II* by Peter Turnbull. The material presented below in chronological order uses all these sources.

As a young teenager in 1945, I was fascinated by stories of training in the United States, each of which had a lesson to be used in life. Discipline and teamwork were part of the airborne culture, and one story in particular impressed me.

During an engineer field training exercise that Tony was conducting as a lieutenant, a jeep got stuck in a deep mud hole. Tony, leading by example, said, "Let's push it out of there," and walked into the mud. A few men followed but most stood on dry ground giving advice and encouragement to those doing the pushing, which eventually got the jeep unstuck.

Tony then had all the men assemble in formation,

and marched them into the mud hole, where he had them mark time march, which is marching in place, until all were wet and filthy. They then marched back to the camp and had no further trouble with discipline or lack of teamwork.

Tony was an excellent shot and was on the rifle team in college. During small arms training at Fort Bragg, one of the men complained that something was wrong with his rifle because he kept missing the target even while using the prone position, which is the easiest. Tony stood off to one side of him, took the rifle, and consistently hit the target from the standing position, the most difficult. The man concluded that he was at fault and not the rifle. The moral I took from this story was that you should look inward before blaming others.

During a massive exercise in Louisiana, Tony told the story of the men getting what they thought was a brilliant idea of positioning themselves in trees in order to more readily see the enemy forces. He told them that it wasn't really a good idea, because once they were in the trees, they couldn't get down without being spotted. Some said that they would stay up a long time, so he let them do it. However, it turned into a blustery cold day, and before long, he had a bunch of chilled, shivering men in the trees. He kept them there until it was safe to come down, and they thought twice before questioning him in the future. The moral I took from this was to think beyond the immediate.

The division went to North Africa in 1943, participated in combat, and prepared for the invasion of Sicily. The only story I remember from Africa was his flying in a test drop of a glider to verify that it could carry a small bulldozer. All turned out well.

I recall no stories about the invasion of Sicily and Italy, where the airborne was used as infantry in slow and bloody combat. This was completely alien to the airborne way of doing warfare, and Tony had nothing good to say about General Mark Clark. Like all the veterans I encountered, Tony did not speak freely about the details of combat.

After the Anzio landing, the division went to England to train for the Normandy invasion. The major things I recall are that the people were friendly and the troops ate a lot of mutton. In fact, they also ate a lot of mutton at Fort Bragg while training in the U.S. and jokingly referred to it as Fort Braaaaaaagg, spoken like the sound of a sheep.

Tony didn't speak much about Normandy, other than mention landing in the Ste. Mere Eglise area and having a close call when he was reconnoitering alone on one side of a hedge row and an enemy patrol took a shot at him from the other side. He claimed that his boyhood deer hunting instincts served him well because he heard the enemy and sprinted across a break in the hedgerow, the bullet barely missing him.

The official records of the 307th Airborne Engineer Battalion, as presented in the Turnbull book, show that, during the airborne drop, his glider landed about 6000 yards east of the planned landing zone, where they made immediate contact with the enemy, and Tony captured four prisoners upon landing.

The battalion commander landed far from the planned area and was immediately captured by the Germans, making Tony, as a captain, the acting battalion commander until a major joined them and took over. The military had a very well-defined chain of command, and someone was always designated to take over when required.

Tony was awarded a Silver Star medal for leading an action to clear a causeway of enemy mines and disabled vehicles while under fire. An enemy shell exploded on one of the disabled vehicles near Tony, but he stood his ground and inspired the men and planned and directed each required task in advance of the troops.

The battalion conducted a variety of combat engineer actions from June 6th until they returned to England in mid July. They had a strength of 24 officers and 280 enlisted men on June 6 and had 18 officers and 195 enlisted on July 9. Of the losses, 10 were killed and the rest missing or wounded.

The battalion took part in the Holland airborne

landing which was the subject of the book and movie *A Bridge Too Far*. Tony wrote some material about this, and it is presented below with only minor editing. The narrative starts before leaving England.

Before we left the field, I placed a sandbag full of sand, that was used as a wheel chock, on the glider seat for protection from FLAK. After I was airborne, I wished that I had another under my feet.

While en route, being able to see C-47s and gliders as far as the eye could see forward and backward was breathtaking. The sight of a C-47 going straight down in a ball of fire was a reminder that this was no picnic.

I was flying in the co-pilot seat of our glider. We were given about one hour of instruction on how to fly one. The summarized advice was to place all controls into neutral and let the glider land itself.

We were so well briefed on our mission that I knew exactly where I was during the whole trip. When I saw our LZ (landing zone) I told the pilot to cut loose from the tow. He just stared in a frozen position. I finally reached up and cut the glider loose when we over the LZ. I told the pilot to turn back for we were headed straight into Germany. It was then that I realized that he had all the controls set in neutral, just like I was advised, and we were going on a one glider invasion of Germany. Later I found out that we would have had company.

I ordered the pilot to make a 180-degree turn, in a command tone. This broke him loose, and he started to put the glider through its gyrations as we made the turn and started to look for a place to land at about 130 miles per hour. We lost one wing on a haystack, then banked and lost the other one on a fence. Without wings our flight ended with the nose of the glider buried in a cultivated field. My feet were also buried.

Seeing ground up to my knees I wasn't sure whether my feet were still a part of me. About that time, an 88 shell landed nearby. I knew the familiar sound of an 88 by now. In nothing flat the jeep, the driver and I were on our way to our designated area. My feet were still with me.

The driver was killed later that afternoon when he went back to look for the 1/4 ton trailer. He was killed by an 88.

There was some humor even in the middle of war. The British were responsible for providing our rations, and after a week of fighting, we received a rum ration. We got a whole week's supply in one day, and we drank it in less than half a day, with astonishing results. After that, we didn't get any more rum.

After about a week, there was a lull in fighting in our area. Not being able to stand this kind of prosperity, John C. H. Lee Jr. and I decided to go look for some glider compasses with which to equip our jeeps. We didn't have much success until we asked some GIs if the gliders we could see at a distance still had compasses. They thought they did.

On foot, we went out to the gliders. We got our compasses.

As we came out of the last glider, we came face to face with a German soldier. The three of us hit the ground. We looked each other over. We decided to go back in our own directions without making any issue out of the situation. John and I didn't run—we did walk fast.

When we came back to the GIs, we asked them if they were an outpost. They said they were. We asked them why they didn't tell us we were at the front line. They said, You didn't ask us about that, you only asked about the compasses.

When the Holland invasion bogged down, the division was withdrawn to rest camps in France. Tony talked some about visiting Paris and staying at the George Cinq Hotel, and being visited by a GI from our village in Pennsylvania. They stayed in the rest areas in France until the Battle of the Bulge, which for them started on December 17, 1944.

Tony didn't talk about this battle at all. However, the activities of the engineer battalion are well documented in the Turnbull book and amounted to blocking the enemy by mining, blowing bridges, and creating obstacles during the enemy advance. When the advance was stopped, they then cleared obstacles, built bridges, and removed mines while U.S. forces advanced. It was during this time that Tony was promoted to major.

The details in the Turnbull book lead one to believe that this was an unending nightmare of activity, with little time for introspection or recording of events. For the battalion, the battle lasted from December 17, 1944 until February 20, 1945, at which time it returned to France for rest. This was a period of over two months of intense combat activity.

On April 2, 1945, the 82nd Airborne returned to combat near Cologne. Tony was in charge of a train convoy of 460 officers and men, who traveled in the *40 and 8 rail cars* of World War I notoriety. After a few days of supporting combat operations, he was temporarily detailed to a special assignment because of his ability to speak Polish. A narrative in Tony's own words follows and covers most of his activities and impressions through the end of the war.

7 April to 18 April

I was camp supervisor for the Etzel camp for displaced persons. The camp was located near Cologne and was one of three set up to place under some control former slave laborers. When placed in charge, I found about 900 Poles, 400 Italians, 200 Hollanders, and 200 miscellaneous nationalities badly organized, living under unsanitary conditions, and fighting over what food was available.

With the aid of two U.S. officers and four Polish liaison officers, I was able to end up with a well-organized camp of about 4000 Poles in about one week—but this took some doing. As a matter of fact, this was one of the most difficult administrative jobs I have ever been assigned—but perhaps the most rewarding.

The kaleidoscopic memories of this period are many.

Endless admissions and transfers . . . resentment of the liberal use of DDT powder . . . steam vat cookers . . . individual servings versus family servings . . . leaking roofs . . . no chlorine in the water . . . short supply of soap . . . 34 weddings on 11 April . . . 130 former PWs acting as guards using 24 weapons without ammunition . . . a 206 enrollment in a kindergarten class and four other children's classes . . . an orchestra for dancing in the corridors . . . demand for passes to equal privileges of German civilians . . . infiltration into camp by German deserters, SS soldiers, and German soldiers . . . rumors of a German parachutist invasion in area . . . organization for rioting . . . a continual search for information about relatives . . .

20 April to 22 April

I was sent over to another displaced persons camp as camp supervisor. I don't recall the name of this one but it contained Poles and Russians and was also located near Cologne.

Here, the UNRRA (United National Relief and Rehabilitation Association) was trying to organize the camp but was having problems. One basic problem was the Poles and

Russians got along like two cats with their tails tied together and thrown over a clothesline. However, an inspection of the camp revealed other problems like a Russian barbecuing two little pigs in a basement to supplement his ration, and all of the displaced persons looked like they were in a flour barrel. It seemed that every time they moved, somebody dusted them with DDT powder.

So, after organizing the mess, dispensary, registration, reception, billeting, etc., the one member of the UNRRA team felt safer than he did when he said, "If it wasn't for the Army, the DPs would eat us for breakfast."

Anyway, UNRRA was left with the remaining problems for we had other irons to put in the fire.

25 April to 29 April

This time was taken up by a slow leisurely trip in a 40 and 8 boxcar from the Cologne area to the Bleckede area near the Elbe River.

30 April

A pontoon bridge was requisitioned from Corps Engineers and was to be built near Bleckede by them during the daylight hours. However, one shell made a direct hit and destroyed two of the pontoons when the bridge was half completed. The bridge construction stopped. This didn't come as a surprise for rear echelon engineers reacted in a similar manner in the past when they heard a shot fired in anger. The bridge was finally completed when a complement of 307th Airborne Engineer Battalion personnel took the initiative in building the bridge.

In the meantime, other engineers from our outfit were manning ducks [DUKW, an amphibious truck] which transported personnel and supplies across the Elbe.

1 May

Immediately after vehicles started to cross the bridge, some of them were mysteriously blown up by large charges of explosives planted in the roadway. This was like nothing comparable to what we have experienced before in North Africa or Europe.

In a search for the cause of the explosions, some suspicious wires were found trenched under the road. A request to stop traffic on the road while further investigation was made was flatly denied. With traffic moving, any investigation was, to say the least, going to be a little shaky.

I personally supervised the disarming of one of these charges and found that a tunnel under the roadway was back-filled with about 250 pounds of explosive and a marine activating device. The activating devices, presumably obtained from the port of Hamburg, were magnetic devices that could be set to trigger the explosive charge after a predetermined number of vehicles (or mine sweepers) safely passed over them. Incidentally, one other team of engineers was blown up while they were attempting to do what our team did.

2 May

With three enlisted men, I went to the village of Belsch to set up a headquarters for the 307th and to find shelter for about 150 personnel. (Belsch was in our assigned defense zone). I contacted the burgomaster of the village and gave him my request. In about a half hour he came back with a list of barns that we could occupy. I advised him that this was not satisfactory. I told him to vacate totally the east half of the village and we would occupy that. I advised him that he had an hour to do so. Much to my surprise he quickly agreed to the proposition. I then sent the jeep driver and one enlisted man back with a message for our outfit to move on up. I kept the interpreter with me in case I needed him.

As soon as the burgomaster put our message on a highly efficient village communication system, we knew that we were going to get more than we bargained for. Among the first people to come out on the street were fully armed German soldiers. This sight coupled with the fact that small arms fire could be heard in the vicinity meant that the interpreter and I had ourselves a village if we could hold it.

We were relieved somewhat when we found out the German soldiers wanted to surrender. We directed them to pile their arms in the center of the village square and to form a group on one corner of the square.

By the time part of our outfit came up, much to our relief, we had about 40 soldiers and one officer in the group. The officer stood out in the group for he was the only one *sitting on a chair. He was a World War I vintage Prussian type Major with a jacket covered with ribbons and medals.*

We directed the group to get aboard the trucks that brought part of our outfit and we would take them back to a PW camp. This the soldiers promptly did. Our distinguished Major remained sitting on the chair with arms folded and demanded he be hauled in a sedan. This was quickly solved when two of our soldiers picked up the chair, Major and all, and set it down on the back of the truck. The trucks took off with one sputtering Major aboard.

The Major did not know that he received a special privilege from us when he was allowed a chair on a truck for this was the last such privilege we passed out. For the rest of the day, so many Germans were surrendering that we just let them go to the rear unguarded, just as they came on foot, trucks, tanks, horses, and bicycles. For two years if you saw a glimpse of a German soldier or vehicle you hit for cover; today you just waved them on to the rear—this sudden change of practice was bewildering.

3 May

I don't think I slept last night or maybe I was sleeping and dreaming all day yesterday. I was quickly assured that yesterday was real for we had so many prisoners that we were running out of drinking water. I went on a mission to try to find some German portable water purification equipment. Which way to go? Naturally the direction the prisoners were coming from—which was from the area held by the 504 and 505 regiments.

The minute the jeep hit the main road I knew this was VE day for me. There was an endless column of soldiers, officers, civilians, prisoners, etc. flowing to the rear like a slow stream passing by the tired, the wounded, the dying, and the dead. I lack words to express this scene, but I vividly remember that I decided that I couldn't have selected a better place to be at the end of the last battle. This was the perfect place to be when you were so full of mixed emotions.

After an hour we arrived at the front line which was clearly identified by a high stack of all types of German weapons. Just fifty feet on the German side were five German officers standing in a group. We approached them. My interpreter started to ask them about the water equipment. Then a tall young German Major said to me, "What is it you want?" in almost perfect English. He assured me that what we were looking for was about two kilometers up the road, but he added, "I would advise you not to go there for some of the others are not in the same mood that we are in." I thanked him for the advice. At this point one of the officers handed me his Luger pistol, which I still have and prize.

The water equipment? We obtained it from our own supply depots.

5 May

I heard about the political prisoner concentration camp located near Ludwigslust. I couldn't believe what I heard so I went to see for myself. The details have been retold many times. These I now believe.

Some of the prisoners that were too weak to walk were still in the camp. Their lack of interest in cigarettes and candy bars that were laying around further describes their condition. I talked to some of them and found them to be intelligent people. The conversation ended abruptly when one of the prisoners said in Polish in a pleading, pathetic tone, "Ja jestem chory (I am sick)." This understatement at this time was too much even for a hardened soldier. (Somehow individual problems are different from the problems of the masses even if they are the same problem.)

7 May

The war is officially over. Thank God.

Tony stayed on in Germany as part of the occupation. There was a rumor that the 82nd Airborne was going to be used in the invasion of Japan, but none of the battle weary veterans had any enthusiasm for that possibility and found it extremely unpleasant after what they had been through. I don't recall Tony speaking at all about the occupation duty.

When the war ended, Tony was 30 years old. He had

traveled a long distance in miles and time from his early years of hoeing potatoes and cutting hay in the small village on the Allegheny Plateau. He had spent about five years in the Army and earned a Silver Star, Bronze Star, and a Croix de Guerre. He had more than enough points to separate, did so, and returned to the States in September of 1945.

He took up his old job as a junior engineer with the electric utility company at the same pay that he had when he was called to active duty in 1940. In a way, it reminds you of the movie *The Best Years of Our Lives*, where the war years and sacrifices counted for nothing once you were back home. However, he was made of stern stuff that had been hardened by his war experiences, so he tackled civilian life and rose through the ranks to become director of engineering for the utility company. He pursued his boyhood passions of trout fishing and deer hunting, and raised a family. He died at the age of 70 from complications resulting from prostate surgery. He was truly one of the Great Generation.

Tony had another major accomplishment for which he received little recognition. He was the first of our family, and indeed the first of the Slavic immigrants' sons, to go off to college. The only encouragement he had for this was from home, and the obstacles he encountered were many. The fellow Slavs looked upon him with suspicion and thought that he was trying to be better than the others. Some of the community, including the doctors, lawyers, and businessmen observed the whole thing with interest as if they were watching a scientific experiment.

The Irish and the Johnny Bulls openly made fun of the idea that a hunky thought he could actually escape "his place in life" and move up in education and status, something that none of them had dared to try. Of all the influences Tony encountered, the negatives, which were frequently hostile, far outweighed the positives. The opportunities to give up were plentiful.

Based on my own experience, Tony showed exceptional fortitude, persevered in the face of all the obstacles, and succeeded. He paved the way for the rest of us, and indeed for the whole Slavic community. What we owe him cannot be expressed in words.

Chapter 33
A New Journey Begins

When the high schools years began, the youth of the plateau began to divide into two groups: those who saw the rest of their lives centered around the same small towns and villages and those who aspired to make their lives in the outside world that was largely unknown to them.

The first group saw life as an extension of that lived by their parents who worked in the coal mines and related industries. They took courses that required little work and were motivated to do even less. The attitude was that "Why should I work hard? It won't count for much in the coal pits." The girls, who saw their big accomplishment in life as getting married after finishing high school, led active social lives.

The relative few in the second group took geometry, higher math, and foreign languages. Serious homework was part of their regimen and being looked down upon by the less motivated was a part of life. However, if you looked deeper, the less motivated were more than a little envious of the adventure that awaited the few.

By few I mean about four. I recall that the four in my senior year trigonometry class were not enough to justify a teacher, so we basically taught ourselves and the most qualified teacher checked our progress about four times during the semester.

College was a further winnowing of the crop. The Presbyterian minister's son and I were the only two who went off to a full-time university—he going to a private liberal arts school and I going to nearby Penn State. Looking back, this was the most important transition in my life, and the four years of college level study, including Air Force ROTC, started me down the less traveled road that Robert Frost so well described. It really did make all the difference.

My interest in airplanes led to a career as an Air Force pilot, aeronautical engineer, and industry vice president. I finally saw most of the world beyond my boyhood village and really did a thousand things that earthbound mortals have not dreamed about.

I frequently go back to my roots on the Allegheny Plateau. From the perspective of my age of ninety, nearly two generations have passed on since the time I was born in my little valley. If I count all the departed that

I knew there, they amount to several hundred in a distance of about two miles, and greatly outnumber those who are left. They made an impact on how life was lived, and except for a few of us older people, none of the current generation is aware of the toil and sweat that they deposited in the place.

If the presence of all those souls were to be felt, it would make a mist of spirituality that would float above the stream and fields and rise and sink with the beginning and end of each day, much like the smoke from the chimneys. Sic transit gloria mundi.

www.ingramcontent.com/pod-product-compliance
Lightning Source LLC
Chambersburg PA
CBHW072002110526
44592CB00012B/1177